A Young Person's Guide to Eventing

Gill Watson
with Lis Clegg

© Gill Watson 1999

A catalogue record of this book is available from the British Library

Edited and produced for The Pony Club
by Barbara Cooper

Designed and typeset by Alan Hamp
Line drawings by Maggie Raynor
Photographs
Cover and p.69: Dr John Julian. Frontispiece: John Mennell/Horse & Hound.
Figs 1, 2, 3, 4, 5, 14, 15, 17a, 18, 19, 20, 36, 40, 41, 42–49, 59, 60, 61, 64,
66, 67, 68, 71: Jane Martindale
16a, b: Foto Factory. 16c, 21: Equestrian Services. 16d: John Britter.
17b Trevor Meeks/Horse & Hound.
39: A. Moesgaard. 56: Shaw-Shot.

ISBN 0-9537167-0-8

The Pony Club
Allander House
NAC Stoneleigh Park
Kenilworth
Warwickshire CV8 2RW
Code: 02476. Tel: 698300 Fax: 696836

Printed and bound in England
by Westway Offset, Wembley

Contents

List of Illustrations

Cover: The author gives instructions to Jenny Julian, a member of the British team who won the gold medal, during the European Junior Championships at Bialy Bor, Poland in 1998.
Frontispiece: Horse trials at Sherborne, Dorset.

Preface

If you aim to become a successful event rider and trainer it is very useful to start young and to have your own ponies, then good horses, on which to learn and gain experience. However, while this is an advantage, it is not essential. Having started to ride at the age of five at the local riding school I had no horse or pony of my own until, at 17 years old, I took the plunge and bought a 12hh Welsh terror to retrain, at the great cost of £20. I progressed through the Pony Club, still on riding school ponies, and competed on any pony which was on offer, in order to gain experience – which all goes to show that you don't need to own the ideal event horse in order to get started.

The Pony Club really provided the key to guidance for the future, and the opportunities to improve riding skills by taking part in all sorts of activities – not least the Prince Philip Cup Mounted Games – helped train my balance, athleticism, horse psychology, courage and determination. At a young age, training is very valuable, but gaining experience by participating and making mistakes along the way is vital, too. I also joined a riding club and rode in riding club teams, so had a good apprenticeship whilst embarking on my first one-day open events.

This book is aimed at helping anyone who is setting out to compete in horse trials, or what is now popularly known as eventing. Competitions are run at many different levels, from Pony Club and Riding Club through to senior events, which begin at pre-novice level. From thinking about your first competition to completing your first three-day event there are a great many potential pitfalls along the way – which you can avoid if you have good guidance from the word go. But above all there are many wonderful things about the sport and, if you set about it in the right way, you will find it both fun and rewarding.

C. Watson

GREAT MISSENDEN 1999

7

1

Introduction

Origins

Horse trials were started by the military as three-day events. A military horse needed great obedience – hence the **dressage**; it needed stamina – hence the **cross-country**; and it needed the suppleness to turn out again after a severe test – hence the **show jumping**. These three disciplines are the basis of the modern three-day event, and they all require athletic ability as well as versatility.

A test was held along these lines in France in 1902. It included dressage, a steeplechase course, roads & tracks and show jumping, but was for military horses only. In 1912 the competition gained Olympic status and at the next Olympics, in Stockholm, Sweden carried away all the honours. After World War Two it was opened to civilians.

The 1948 Olympics were held in England, with the three-day event steeplechase phase at Tweseldown and the roads & tracks and cross-country on Barossa Common, behind the Royal Military Academy at Sandhurst. The British team did not do particularly well, so a year later the Duke of Beaufort initiated Badminton Horse Trials with a view to giving our riders a chance to practise for the next Olympics. Since then the interest in three-day eventing in Great Britain has continued to grow.

The first official one-day events were held in 1950 at Hallyburton (Central Scotland) and Great Auclum (Berkshire). A half-century later the sport is not only flourishing throughout the country but is still expanding.

Why go eventing?

There are so many attractions to this sport, and different people have different reasons for taking part (it certainly isn't the money, since eventing is still way behind show jumping in the prize and sponsorship stakes). It is a very accessible sport – at the lower levels a good family horse can do well, and if you're not brilliant at one phase, you can often make up points on another. Each phase complements the next: once the horse becomes more supple and athletic in his dressage work, then he finds it easier to jump; and once he is better disciplined, then control on the cross-country improves. With three different challenges in one competition and lots of scope for family and friends to get involved too, there's something for everyone.

With more space than the average small show where everyone is crammed into one field, and less milling around because competitors know their start times, events are far less chaotic than other shows. Knowing what time you are performing is a great help, because you can plan your day to have enough warm-up time and as little waiting as possible. As well as being best for your horse, this gives you less time to get nervous.

You don't even have to ride

Events are usually held in lovely surroundings, often parkland that would not otherwise be open to the public. There is plenty of space for everyone and non-riders can get involved, too: for example as fence judges. Fence judging can be fascinating as you watch how different riders tackle your particular jump. You can learn all about it by starting with someone who knows the job; then eventually you will be able to do it yourself, beginning with the briefing which all fence judges attend before the cross-country. It's a great way to meet new friends and of course there's the chance to go shopping at the trade stands in between classes.

Some fence judges and other officials become so experienced and well-known in the sport that they get invited to help at foreign events, even European and World Championships and the Olympics. So even if you're not the world's greatest rider, you could still be there.

A little bit of bureaucracy

If you are under 21 it is a good idea to join the Pony Club. Members may be up to 18 years old, then Associate Members are from 18 to 21 years old. The Pony Club has a central committee, which runs the overall system, and the country is divided into regional branches, which all have a District Commissioner and a committee to run them. Each branch plans a programme to suit all ages and stages, and there are branches in both rural and urban areas.

Riding Clubs are run in a similar manner, and both Pony Club and Riding Clubs often use British Horse Trials Association (BHTA) courses for their competitions. Riding Club members must generally be 17 or over, although some clubs now take junior members.

The opportunities that these two organisations offer for gaining general riding experience, both mounted and unmounted, as well as experience of hunting, polo and the competitive disciplines, are all highly valuable to the potential event rider. In the UK, one-day events begin at Pony Club level, so anyone who is a member can compete. Teams and individuals can work their way up from their first competition to area events and, ultimately, the Pony Club One-Day Event Championships. You will be eligible to compete in competitions run by both your own and other branches, which means ultimately that you can compete against – and get to know – other members from all over the country, which helps make the day more enjoyable.

Other organisations of which you need to be aware are the FEI (Federation Equestre Internationale) and the BHTA or the equivalent national organisation in your country. The FEI is the international governing body of equestrian sport. Based in Lausanne, Switzerland, it is responsible for the running of all international competitions.

National rules are based roughly on FEI rules, though they may vary between different countries and levels. Generally, three-day events are run under FEI rules, while one-day events are run under national rules. The BHTA is the governing body for eventing in Britain. Its responsibilities range from registering riders, owners and horses to organising locations for events and handling the financial side. It also selects and organises training for teams who represent their country both at home and abroad.

Getting started

By walking courses and talking to other competitors about courses over which they have competed, you begin to find out which competitions will be useful to help you increase your experience. 'L' fences are often provided at Pony Club competitions for less experienced horses or riders, offering simpler routes by which to negotiate the more demanding fences. At this level you will not need the highest quality horse to cope, but once you decide to move on you need a greater degree of commitment. So much can go wrong in eventing that you need to know exactly what you are getting into. If the riders, let alone the horses, are unfit and not up to the job then the sport becomes dangerous for all concerned.

Most competitions have upper and lower age limits – for the rider, not the horse! – but there is plenty of overlap, so you're not limited to just one category. Competitions are run over all heights and types of cross country course, from the 2ft 3in Mini to the 3ft 6in Open courses. The Pony Club normally uses its own dressage tests, while Riding Clubs generally use BHTA or BHS tests. Some Riding Club competitions are open to non-members, but to qualify for the national final you need to be a member. You may be chosen to represent your branch of Pony Club or Riding Club at Area level. Different branches within your allocated area compete against each other with teams of three or four people, and if your team comes first or second then it qualifies for the National Championships, which are held every year. The Area level for both Pony Club and Riding Club is equivalent to a strong Novice course, with the show jumping at a maximum of 3ft 9in. The championships are tougher, but often there are easier or longer alternative routes so a Novice horse can get round without terrifying itself – or its rider. However, you should aim to have educated yourselves enough to be confident of a good ride.

BHTA-affiliated competitions

When you have gone clear across country over PC or RC Open 3ft 6in horse trials courses, you are probably ready to start BHTA Pre-Novice Horse Trials. Horse trials run by the BHTA are known as 'affiliated' competitions and riders and horses must all be registered with the BHTA. Horses must also be registered on the British Horse Database, a national record of data covering history, performance and breeding. Similar systems operate all over the world so wherever you are competing, make sure that you have a copy of that country's official rules.

Under BHTA rules, horses win points each time they are placed in an event above pre-novice level, and these points determine which grade they can compete in. For example, once a horse has won a points at novice or gained a certain number at another level, he will have to move up a class or compete *hors concours* (HC) at the lower level. You can, however, compete in as many pre-novice events as you like, as no points are awarded at this level. The figures we give in this book are correct at the time of going to press but they may change, so always check in the current Rule Book. The system can seem rather complicated until you get used to it.

Counting the days

One-day events run all the phases on the same day. But even in one-day events, if there are a lot of entries you may have to do your dressage the day before.

Two-day events provide an introduction to the format of a three-day event. Dressage and show jumping are held on day one, with speed and endurance (roads & tracks, steeplechase and cross-country) on day two.

Three-day events are divided into star categories, from one-star * to four-star ****. Make sure that you understand what standard you need to achieve for each level, so that you have time to qualify. In three-day events the dressage is on day one (sometimes day two as well), the speed and endurance phases are on the day after the dressage, and the show jumping is on the final day. If there are a lot of entries the event may take up more than three days.

You will find a more detailed explanation in Chapters 10 and 11.

2

Starting Out – What you Need

Almost anyone can event, though the sport tends to be associated with younger riders because of its physical demands. The oldest winner at Badminton so far was 46 years old and the youngest 18, but plenty of competitions offer scope for a wider range of ages and abilities. Whether you are an aspiring professional or an enthusiastic amateur who is happy to compete in spite of other commitments such as school, college, work or family, you need to assess your goals, match them up with your lifestyle and set yourself a realistic target. Know your limits. Don't be over ambitious, as it will only land you in trouble; but, equally, learn how far you can push yourself to get that extra level of performance. You also need to learn how to keep motivated through the peaks and troughs of success and failure.

Your age, level of experience and the amount of time you can devote to practising are bound to influence your decisions. Competing is a time-consuming business, from looking after the horse and putting in the training to the day of the event itself. While you are at school it is relatively easy to fit the horse around your studies, but at college or when you start work it becomes more difficult and you may have to take a break from serious competing to concentrate on exams. Don't ignore these factors – if you intend to remain amateur, you will need to finance your hobby and if you turn professional, you may find yourself running an equestrian business or retiring from competition at an age when you still need to work. Several equestrian college courses now include business studies, a useful skill to have.

Physical fitness is important at every level – think how out-of-breath you can get just having a normal lesson if you are unfit. There is little point in the horse being supremely fit if the rider becomes exhausted half way round the course and stops riding effectively; a fit body is also less prone to injury and, if you do get injured, has a faster recovery rate.

If you have already competed in other disciplines you will find it

1. One way of getting fit close to home.

easier to start eventing, not least because you know what it's like to perform in front of judges and spectators. You will also have learnt some 'ring craft' and be familiar with the competitive environment. If you have not competed before, take some time to watch competitions. Go as a groom to someone who is competing, read books and watch videos on the subject, and ask experienced competitors for help and advice. However challenging a course may look, sheer guts alone will not get you round in one piece – you also need to use your common sense and ride intelligently.

When you start competing, find the right level for yourself so that you do not jump in at the deep end and overface yourself or your horse. Pony Club or Riding Club events are ideal, as are hunter trials, since they will provide small (but not necessarily too easy) courses, and most of the other competitors will be at a similar level to yourself. Never be afraid to ask more experienced competitors for advice – they are usually very happy to help. Once you are safe and confident at a particular level, you can think about moving up.

Do you need help?

Eventing is a tough sport and it's difficult to go it alone. Having someone to train you is a great advantage. The trainer does not have to be well-known or someone you can only afford now and again. It is far better to establish a regular working relationship with someone you get on with, whose methods suit you and who will be there for advice and backup when you need it. Many riding clubs organise one-off training sessions with 'big names' which you can take part in or watch, and if you are selected for a team you will have a chance to work with the team trainer. It is also a great help to have someone – preferably experienced – on the ground to give helpful advice, move jumps and generally lend a hand. At competitions, having someone there to discuss the course, put up the practice fence, collect numbers and fetch coffee can make all the difference when you're under pressure.

What facilities are necessary?

Keeping a horse at or very near your home is ideal, if you can manage it. The stable should be at least 12ft x 12ft (3.5 x 3.5 metres); you will also need somewhere to turn the horse out, plus access to a suitable area for schooling. If you don't have the time or the your own facilities, it may be better to keep him at a professional yard where he can be properly cared for and where there are suitable exercise and training facilities on site. This can be expensive, but it has the advantage of expert backup being on hand if you need it.

2. The author's yard at Hyde Farm West, Great Missenden.

For most private owners one acre per horse is enough for turnout if the horse is mainly stabled, but it is not a substitute for exercise. Turning out horses in a strange environment may be fraught with dangers. Horses who are relaxed at home or with a familiar companion may get into mischief and injure themselves in an unfamiliar field with more horses around. Horses are quite adaptable and can always be led out for a short graze every day, provided they are given enough exercise.

Hacking is important, too, and hilly countryside is useful for fitness work. Roads can be hazardous, so if you *have* to use them try to avoid busy commuter times and make sure that you are familiar with the *Highway Code*. For schooling and jumping, a flat surface of at least 20 x 40 metres is desirable. This gives you enough space to work satisfactorily and is the size of the smallest dressage arena in which you are likely to compete. If you are lucky enough to be on naturally well-drained, sandy soil you may be able to work in the corner of a field, or to construct an arena quite easily; otherwise you will need a special all-weather surface. Don't despair if you can't have your own sandschool, as someone near by may have one that you can use. Be prepared to pay or help out in return.

3. Working in the sandschool, Hyde Farm West.

Everyday equipment

We will deal with clothing for competitions in Chapter 9, but for every-day work, rider and horse both need to be dressed for comfort and safety. The main rule for tack is that it MUST FIT and be kept in good

4. Correct turnout for everyday work.

condition, with regular checks of stitching on leather – especially girth straps, stirrup-leathers and reins. Tack doesn't have to be complicated and you don't need lots of gadgets.

Initially a general purpose saddle will see you through, until you feel ready to progress to different saddles for each discipline. Leg protection for the horse is very important. Take care when choosing boots – they must fit the horse when he's in action, not just standing still. Make sure that they don't rub or restrict movement. See Chapter 9.

For the rider, a hard hat is essential at all times. The minimum safety standards in the UK at the time of writing are PAS 015, BSEN 1384 or ASTM SEI 1163. You have to wear a hard hat for all jumping disciplines, with a black or navy cover for show jumping and your own colours for the cross-country.

Safe footwear is vital: for example, boots should have a small heel. Of course, at home you can ride in jeans, but jodhpurs or breeches give you more comfort and movement. Chaps or half-chaps can be worn, but beware when they get old as they can rub the horse's sides. Gloves help protect your hands and are particularly vital for lungeing.

The Horse

Do you need your own horse?

When you start out you can have a lot of fun competing on borrowed horses or ponies, but as you progress it can prove very difficult to get rides, even at pre-novice level. Once you reach the senior levels of the Pony Club and decide to move on from ponies it is time to think of the future, and having your own horse gives you more control over your decisions.

If you are aiming for the top, will your horse take you there? At this stage you have a choice between buying a more experienced horse who will give you confidence but may not take you beyond a certain level, or a young horse to bring on who is capable of taking you to the top. Be honest with yourself about your goals and your capabilities, and gain experience from horses who are already trained before you set out to train one yourself. Everyone makes mistakes at first, so if possible go for a horse with a forgiving temperament.

To be successful takes a huge amount of time and commitment. You must get to know the horse inside out, from his abilities and temperament to his appetite and every lump and bump on his legs, so that you notice if something is not quite right and you are prepared to face difficult

5. Good Pony Club-type event horse with rider.

situations. Then you can use all this knowledge to set the right training programme.

What type of horse do you need?

The important points when you choose an event horse are: temperament; soundness (and conformation); athletic ability; age; type and breeding; and whether it's suitable for the rider. This doesn't mean that the horse you already have won't take you eventing – in fact as long as you both have the ability and confidence, it is probably your best bet for starting out. Plenty of quite ordinary horses are successful at hunter trials and local or novice one-day events, but as you move up the scale you will need a horse who can cope with the extra demands. All-round ability, stamina and good schooling can go a long way in eventing. Though jumping and dressage abilities are important, event horses don't have to reach the same standards as top level show jumpers or dressage horses, but they certainly need more stamina. Many good eventers were originally racehorses or show jumpers who didn't quite make the grade.

Temperament

Temperament is really important. We work with our horses every day, so it is much easier and more fun if they are nice characters. First impressions are useful. Take note of how a horse greets you, what he's like to handle, whether he tries to please when you ride him, whether he's happy to leave the yard and other horses, and whether he's happy to work both on his own and in a group. You can tell a lot about a horse by his eyes – for example, good, honest eyes set wide apart often indicate a temperament to match. Many people like to see a 'Prophet's thumbprint', a little groove like a thumbprint on the neck, because the traditional belief (which stems from Arabia) that it signifies an honest horse often turns out to be true.

6. Prophet's thumbmark.

21

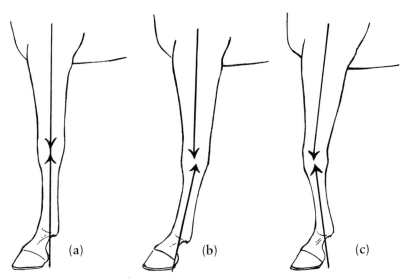

7. *Foreleg conformation, side view: (a) correct, (b) back at the knee,
(c) over at the knee.*

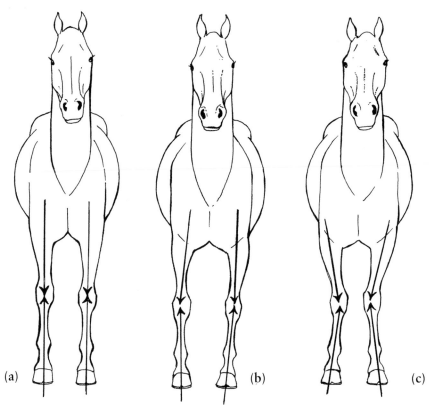

8. *Foreleg conformation, front view: (a) correct, (b) bow-legged, (c) knock-kneed.*

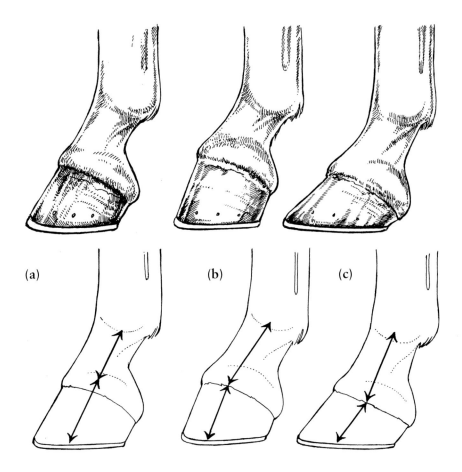

9. *Shape of foot: (a) correct angle of pastern and hoof; well-shaped hoof, (b) too upright; boxy hoof, (c) angle and hoof too flat.*

Soundness and conformation

Many shapes and sizes of horse make good eventers, but certain conformation weaknesses can lead to problems. On the other hand, perfect conformation does not guarantee good performance, so you really need to use your own (or your adviser's) judgment.

Some useful points to look for:

• Short cannon bones are normally strongest.

• An eventer needs 'good bone', which basically means that his legs should look strong enough to support his body.

• Straight front legs. Being 'back at the knee', when the legs below the knees look narrow, often leads to strains. Being 'over at the knee' is less likely to cause problems.

• The bone of the knee and fetlock joints should be flat and not too rounded.

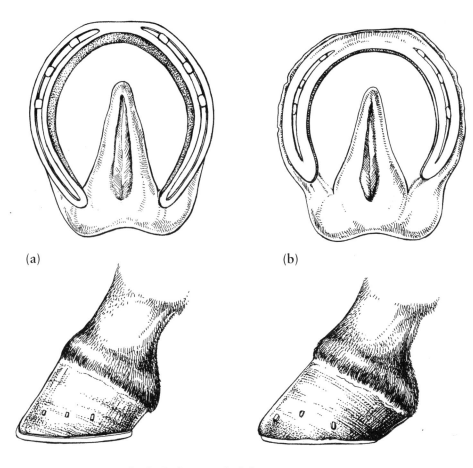

10. Foot: (a) correctly shod, (b) in need of shoeing.

• Look at the angle of the pastern. Too upright can lead to jarring and too sloping may be weak.

• Look for good, evenly shaped feet that are in proportion to the horse and to each other. The often-quoted saying 'No foot, no horse' is quite true. The hoof should be at the same angle as the pastern and should have sound walls, as brittle feet can cause shoeing problems. Small, boxy feet can lead to later trouble such as navicular.

• Does the horse move straight? If he turns a toe in, it's likely to keep hitting the opposite leg. Turning toes out is less of a problem as long as the leg is not set on crooked. The hind legs should be powerful, with strong hocks that flex well and allow the horse to plant its hind feet well under its body.

• Length of back. Long backs may be weaker, but many good jumpers have them.

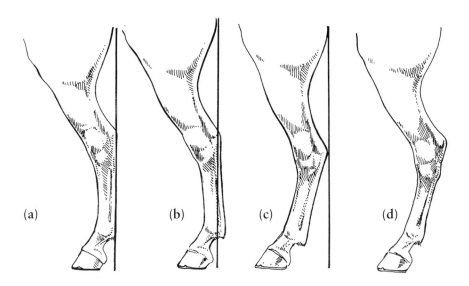

11. Hind legs, side view: (a) correct, (b) out behind, (c) angle too acute, (d) sickle-hocked.

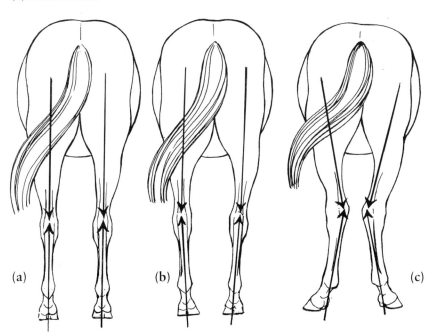

12. Hind legs, back view: (a) correct, (b) bow-legged, (c) cow-hocked.

• A good, sloping shoulder indicates that the neck is set on well, so the horse will be able to carry himself more easily. High withers are not a conformation fault but can cause problems with saddle-fitting.

*13. Shoulder conformation: (a) good,
sloping shoulder, (b) too upright.*

Type and age

Finding a horse to suit you is a matter of personal preference: for example, some people love riding Thoroughbreds while others are not so keen on them, and some people prefer geldings to mares. If you're 5ft tall, try not to fall for a 17hh horse!

How you intend to keep the horse is important, too. If it has to live out during the winter, a halfbred or Irish horse will cope better than a Thoroughbred. Thoroughbred types are generally 'sharper' so are less suitable for inexperienced riders. A less highly bred horse may not seem as exciting, but he will be easier to manage, will give you more confidence and can be just as successful.

The horse's age, too, will depend on your experience and how much time you have. If you are experienced, starting with a three- or four-year-old horse can work well, but for novices, or if you have less time, an older, more experienced horse is far better. There is one snag, though – horses accumulate points as they move up through the BHTA levels and once they have a certain number, they have to move up to the next level. So an experienced horse might already have too many points for the level at which you want to compete, which means you would only be able to ride HC at that level.

A four-year-old horse who has been well educated will not have much

Top 14. *Good pony-type eventer.*   Above 15. *Half-warmblood eventer.*

experience, nor will he have had time to develop bad habits, but at that age he will soon develop them if you allow him to. At six, he should have competed a little and 'seen the outside world'. Eight years old is an excellent age, as the horse has already gained experience and should not lose his value over the next couple of years. Be careful when buying from a professional, as a horse may look easy when they ride him but turn out to be more difficult than you thought. Do be honest about your experience, or lack of it.

Athletic ability

Loose-limbed horses – i.e. those who move freely with a 'loose', uncramped action – are usually athletic. A good walk and canter are important, and a good trot is helpful. Watch the horse being ridden on both reins so that you can see whether he goes equally well each way. Ask yourself if he has presence and agility and carries himself well. Then watch him jumping. Look at the shape he makes over the fence and whether he powers himself from speed or athleticism – and does he enjoy the task? Ride the horse yourself and think about how he feels, as well as how he performs. Consider whether he's the right size, weight and width for you, since you're the one who will be riding him. Don't be too influenced by flashy movement or over-jumping.

How to find a suitable horse

Word of mouth is the best way. Look at adverts in magazines, but however impressively they read you will need to ask a lot of questions when you phone up. Check out previous experience, temperament and soundness, and any other points which occur to you. Don't be shy. When you go to see a horse, take along an experienced adviser who knows *you*, as well as what to look for objectively in a horse; even if you're quite experienced, a second opinion is helpful. Be honest about your ability and what you will want the horse to do; otherwise you are wasting each other's time. Always have a horse vetted before you buy it and, depending on its price and level, you may want the vet to take X-rays as well. If the vendor says the horse has horse trials points, check this with the BHTA or your country's governing body.

3

Planning your Progress

There are four age levels at which you may be eligible to compete in affiliated horse trials.
Pony Riders (13 to 16 years, ponies 148cm or under)
Junior Riders (15 to 18 years, horses over 148cm)
Young Riders (19 to 21 years, horses over 148cm)
Senior Riders (all ages over 16 years, horses over 148cm)

From each group a team is selected to represent your country at international level. To be considered for Pony, Junior and Young Rider teams, you need to read the BHTA's Omnibus Schedule to establish the standard of competition and how to qualify. Each age group invites applications for trials from any rider qualified at the right level. The trials are held throughout the country and overseen by committees who monitor not only the results but how the results are achieved. It is important to select riders who have a high degree of skill rather than the brave but kamikaze rider who will ultimately end up on the ground.

Riders who are considered to be of a suitable standard then go forward to further selection procedures. Juniors and Young Riders go to separate three-day events, after which a shortlist is drawn up. This is followed by a final trial and team selection. The teams consist of four team riders and two individuals, and they compete at different venues in Europe in late summer each year.

For the Ponies a similar system is used, with partnerships qualifying by completing at least three one-day events at 3ft6in with clear runs across country. These competitions may include Pony Club Area Horse Trials in the previous year. Selection is very strict, and those considered suitable will then be offered a Pony Trial, of which there are currently only three throughout the UK. From these, 40 riders are selected to compete at a final trial at the end of May/early June.

The European Championships for Pony Riders are usually held in July,

16. Four pictures showing progress up the levels of eventing:
(a) Fun and determination at the first stage.

and five riders are chosen – four in the team, plus one individual. In the autumn after these championships, potential team members for the following year may be invited to compete at a friendly International event, where they will have the opportunity to gain further experience.

(b) Concentration as the fences get bigger.

Where to begin

The level of your own and your horse's experience will dictate where you can start competing. It will take time to form a secure partnership where you both have confidence in one another, and competing too soon at too high a level may well cause either you or the horse to lose your nerve.

Once you have moulded a good relationship it is time to become more ambitious and make a longer term plan: i.e. look at your main aim for the year and arrange your schedule accordingly. It is important to find out how to go about qualifying for the competitions that you have in mind and decide whether these are realistic goals. Then build up a programme of one-day events, making sure that you will gain enough experience along the way without over-running the horse.

There are so many events to choose from that you should make careful plans well in advance. You must take into consideration:
1. The age and experience of your horse
2. Your own availability to compete
3. The distance you are prepared to travel
4. Any other events for which you are aiming to qualify.

(c) Achievable skills at a young age.

(d) The rider from photo (a) five years on, at a Novice event.

A young horse needs to gain general experience by competing in all phases individually at first, so go to some dressage and show jumping competitions, as well as hunter trials and cross-country training sessions. Once he is ready you can embark on his first one-day event, which will be mentally and physically quite testing. You must allow him time to learn from his experiences; and even if he happens to go very well, don't be misled into thinking that he is instantly ready for more. Initially, once a fortnight for perhaps three pre-novice events will be constructive, and if he is coping well and full of confidence he will gain useful experience. If he is struggling, however, be prepared to go back to basics and sort out minor problems before they become major ones.

When you decide to enter your first pre-novice event it makes sense to seek advice from an experienced competitor, as courses can vary considerably. Initially, check the BHTA Bulletin and Omnibus Schedule for advice as to the severity of courses and the type of going. Some courses state whether they are suitable for first-timers, and it is preferable to start when the ground conditions are favourable.

After three events you can assess whether to leave a few weeks, then go to a couple more pre-novices before progressing to novice level. The more experience you can get at lower levels, the easier it will be when you move up a grade. Once your horse is ready, the same sort of plan goes for novice level. Here you can run about once a fortnight – but if the programme and travelling distance are such that you sometimes have to compete two weeks running, be careful to leave a couple of free weeks, or more if necessary, for the horse to recharge and get his stress levels down.

Once you have made a confident start you can progress to planning a programme for your horse to aim towards qualifying for some bigger events. You may be worried about doing this, so work out how far you can push yourself, but do not be led into aiming beyond your wishes or capabilities. The most important fact to remember is the reason why you are doing all this – it should be for achievement, improvement and, above all, fun.

For those looking to upgrade horses, you must study the BHTA Omnibus Schedule carefully early in the year and decide what you need to

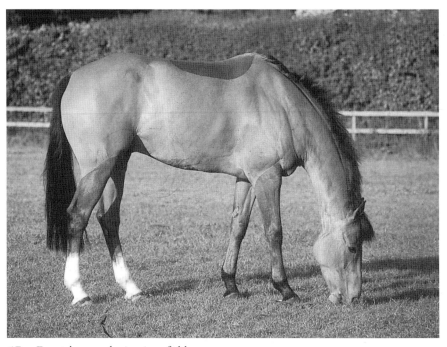

17a. Event horse relaxing in a field.

17b. *Three former Young Riders who went on to great things: (left to right) Tina Gifford, Pippa Funnell (née Nolan) and Jeanette Brakewell, with team-mate Ian Stark, winning the senior team gold medal in the 1999 European Championships at Luhmühlen, Germany. Pippa also won individual gold.*

do to qualify for your aims. Officially there are three seasons – spring, summer and autumn, extending from March to October, with no break in between. This does not mean that you should run every two weeks. You must plan your events ahead, but be flexible and prepared to re-route if necessary. Horses vary in the number of runs they need: once a fortnight is possible for a few runs; up to ten to twelve a year is plenty. Then consider a three-day event if you are aiming that high and are sufficiently prepared. All plans will be influenced by:

- Your horse's condition
- His performance
- His fitness
- His soundness
- The enjoyment factor for both of you, but especially for the horse.

We will go into more detail on fitness programmes in the next chapter, but remember that holidays for horses are just as much a mental break as a physical one. The competitions themselves are not all that tiring for the horse, but the general fitness and training programmes take their toll. I do not believe that horses need long breaks, but two or three weeks with no schooling and the freedom of the field can work wonders and will not be long enough for the horse to lose fitness or to forget his progress.

Do remember that turning a horse out when the grass is lush must be done carefully. If your horse is used to going in the field daily, you can quite quickly increase the time he is out. If, however, he has been stabled during his training period, his move from stable to field must be gradual so that his digestive system has time to adjust. Horses are creatures of habit, and you may also find that a horse accustomed to living in will not be happy left in the field for too long.

4

Fitness

Getting your horse fit is a long, slow process. Although a novice event horse doesn't need to be as fit as a racehorse, he does need all-round strength and stamina, so from your unfit horse to a novice event takes about 12 weeks of consistent work. You are aiming to have the horse – and yourself – fit enough to go for approximately five minutes (a pre-novice event is run at 490 metres per minute, a novice at 520 m/min, and the courses are usually about 1,600 to 2,800 metres in length). As you go up through the grades the running time becomes faster, so you need to be that much fitter.

When you first bring the horse in from a holiday in the field, you will need to walk him on flat, firm ground for about four weeks to harden his legs and prepare his heart and lungs. After that he will be ready to trot and to gradually increase the work. This may sound boring when you're itching to event, but cutting corners really will lead to problems and injuries. A horse-walker can be helpful, but it is best used in addition to, rather than instead of, the fitness work.

When you introduce schooling, remember that the horse will find it tiring until he has developed enough muscle, so now start building his stamina and improving his heart and lung capacity. Do enough work to stress him a little but NEVER to strain him. Slow hacking up and down hills is a brilliant way to strengthen both his body and his lungs and when you start canter work, slow canters up a slope will work wonders. Do make sure that you are balanced and sitting still in the saddle so that the horse can cope with what you ask of him. A tired rider bumping about in the saddle will cause all sorts of problems, from saddle sores to unbalanced horses knocking and possibly laming themselves.

During this build-up you can enter plenty of small competitions to help keep both you and the horse interested, and to gauge your progress. Try to plan your fitness programme so that the horse is challenged but not worn out. Two or three serious dressage sessions a week are enough for

18. *Unfit small Advanced horse.*

19. *Unfit horse: too round, muscles not tuned.*

20. Fit horse showing good muscle tone, not carrying excess weight, skin sleek and supple.

most horses, but you can still be schooling while you're out hacking – for example by working up to the bridle, leg-yielding along a nice wide path or bending round trees. But remember, constant nagging will bore the horse very quickly. He must be allowed to enjoy his work.

Jump training is important, as it helps the horse to use the correct muscles in his back and to keep his eye in; also, it's fun for both of you. Hacking in interesting countryside is both useful and enjoyable, but do try to use roads, too, if you can – though not at busy commuter times. Be polite to motorists and show your appreciation when they slow down. Even if your horse isn't scared of traffic he might shy at something in the hedge, and motorists don't always realise how quickly a horse can dart sideways.

A young horse initially takes longer to reach peak fitness, as an older horse generally retains a certain level of fitness even after a holiday. In general, horses are better with not too long a lay-off.

Sometimes two to three weeks in summer is enough, with probably a longer break of four to six weeks at the end of the season. Remember – in order to progress you need time to teach your horse, so think ahead and allow yourself sufficient training time before and between competitions.

Your fitness programme will depend on the situation prevailing before you start. A grossly overweight horse who has had a long lay-off will be profoundly different from one who was in competition fitness two months earlier. A horse constantly walking in the field requires less time than a stabled horse returning from injury, whose work has to be started gradually and monitored carefully. Slopping along on exercise is not valuable.

Sample fitness programme

Week One
If the horse has been turned out and taking a reasonable amount of exercise in the field, then he will be easier to start in work than one who has been confined to a stable. The change from field to work must be made gradually and you can help make it less dramatic by doing the initial walking exercise from the field, if possible. Before you start, make sure that the horse has:

- His feet checked and shod
- Annual injections up to date
- His teeth checked

Worming is usually best left until he is stabled, but if he will still be turned out in the field every day he can be wormed before you start the work programme.

During this first week he would be better on two shorter walk sessions a day of 30mins each rather than one long one. Be careful, especially if he is very fat and soft, that his tack does not rub, particularly around the girth area; sores and rubs at this stage can hold up progress.

Walking on flat roads is preferable, although gentle hills will do no harm. Often when first into work a horse is quiet, and stress and tiredness should be avoided, but as he gets fitter and stronger so he becomes naughtier. Be careful on roads, and try to take a sensible 'babysitter' with a youngster. It is good if the horse can also spend time in the field during this period so that he does not become unsafe to walk out.

Feeding must progress with work, but be careful to keep the work ahead of the feed – that is, only increase the feed once the horse's workload has increased.

Week Two
Continue the walking, build up the length of time from 1hr to 1hr 30mins and start gradual hills if available.

Weeks Three and Four

As horses are creatures of habit, you do not want suddenly to change their whole routine when you start competing. Continue to walk, finding steeper hills when possible, and continue to turn out, but for shorter spells. This helps the horse to become accustomed to living in the stable, and prevents him overeating grass in the early spring and summer. As long as the horse is sound and not recovering from an injury, it is advisable to trot for short spells, as he may well begin to misbehave when he starts to feel fitter, and will need more exercise.

Week Five

Progress with trotting, at first on the flat, then on hills, but keep up the walking too. If your horse is now mainly confined to the stable, if possible work him twice a day – 1hr 30mins in the morning and 30mins in the afternoon. Some schooling can also start, such as circles in walk and trot with transitions.

Week Six

Schooling can continue. Keep up the hacking, but introduce more schooling, being careful to work on both reins. Use trotting poles to maintain interest.

Week Seven

Progress with schooling including canter. Start jumping. Increase time spent in the school, but continue hacking.

Week Eight

Continue dressage and jump training. The horse should now be stronger and more muscular. Keep up his interest with some longer canters when hacking.

Week Nine

Continue dressage and jump training. Introduce some small competitions. Build up cantering when hacking and in the arena.

Week 10

Introduce cantering twice a week. If on hilly going there is no need, with a novice horse, to go fast. Canter with short stirrups in order to train your lower leg and improve your balance.

Week 11

By now the horse should feel fit and well, and your general fitness programme must continue. However, any fast work from now on will depend on your long-term aim. If you are heading for a pre-novice or novice one-day event, you do not need to reach the peak of fitness. Just find a level at which the horse can easily canter for five minutes without becoming stressed. It is better to maintain a level of fitness which you can retain for quite a long time than to reach one which cannot be maintained.

Week 12

By now your horse should be ready to go round his first event. You do not need him to be gaining more fitness at this level, so the occasional short break from schooling, with time in the field, will be a useful mental and physical relaxation for him. Do not rest him by shutting him in the stable, as this will lead to other problems.

5

The Disciplines

Dressage

This phase is a test of the horse's obedience, suppleness, accuracy, balance and rhythm. Ultimately a well trained horse should appear in harmony with the rider and should be sufficiently relaxed to show off his paces to the best of his ability. The demands of this phase increase as the experience and development of horse and rider progress.

Dressage tests are written in order to encourage correct training of the horse. They start with the basic paces of walk, trot and canter, and transitions. Initially, transitions can be progressive (for example, from walk to canter via trot, rather than straight into canter) but as the level becomes higher so the tests become more demanding and require differences within the paces – working, medium and extended – plus lateral movements and direct transitions (i.e. from walk straight into canter).

In horse trials, dressage tests are lettered A, B, C and so on to signify the degree of difficulty, and the Omnibus Schedule tells you which tests are required at each event. There are several tests for each level so do study the rules for the particular level at which you are competing, as there are some differences in tack allowed between horse trials and pure dressage (in the UK, the BHTA Rule Book will give you this information). Another rule states at what level spurs are compulsory; initially they are optional. In most novice tests the trot work can be executed in rising trot, but this will be written on your copy of the test.

Each phase of an event is related to the others, so the dressage training must have the jumping very much in mind.

The paces

Event horses come in many shapes and sizes and are not chosen for their paces, so there is bound to be a wide variety, some with naturally good movement, others less fortunate. It is an advantage if the horse happens to have correct paces, but it is not essential. Temperament, athleticism and jumping ability are of primary importance to the event horse.

21. *Pony rider showing extended paces.*

Below, 22. *The walk: four-time sequence.*

(a) (b)

The walk

It is often said that when looking for a winner in the paddock at a race meeting, go for a horse with a good walk – long, easy strides covering plenty of ground – as this signifies that he will be able to gallop. This is not just an old wives' tale and is a good point to note when looking for your perfect horse. The walk is a four-time rhythm which must not be destroyed by tension or hurrying. The *medium walk* required in novice dressage tests requires an even, light contact from the rider's hand to the horse's mouth, with the horse accepting the bit and taking it forward in even, purposeful steps. If he is lazy and strolls along you will need to encourage a more purposeful approach, but beware of hurrying and therefore shortening the strides. The horse may jog when he is tense or when the rider is anxious and hurries the steps.

Free walk is also required at novice level. This requires a long rein but not a loose one. The difference is that with a loose rein the rider has no contact with the horse's mouth, just a looping rein, and often the horse will be inactive and hollow. A long rein is exactly that – you allow the horse to stretch and take the rein forward as much as possible. In doing so he should stretch the muscles along the top of his body and lower his neck, thus allowing the strides to lengthen. It is important to practise the transitions from free walk to medium walk and vice versa, so that the horse remains calm and does not jog or feel restricted or pressured by medium walk, causing him to snatch the reins as a means of escape for free walk – which is not the intention!

The more advanced your horse becomes, the greater the degree of difficulty in the tests, which then include the *extended walk*. The rider asks the horse to take longer steps and stretch forward with head and neck, maintaining a light contact on the rein, similar to free walk but without going as low. Be careful not to push too much, which will hustle the rhythm.

● (c)   (d) ●

23. *The free walk:*
(a) correct, long and low,
(b) incorrect, dropped contact.

(a)

(b)

In *collected walk*, the horse shortens his steps but maintains the rhythm and activity so that his steps are a little higher. Be careful not to cause tension by too much pressure or just slow the steps, as both faults will go towards destroying the horse's natural gait. Walk movements can often be improved by teaching him to move away from the leg in walk, using turns on the forehand, half-pirouettes and leg yielding. Collected walk is not used in FEI tests, but it can be useful in training.

The trot

Trot is a two-time pace which can vary greatly in horses according to their differing conformation. Short striding and rather pottering trot steps are a disadvantage, but trotting is not the most important pace in a jumping horse. I was once teaching a young steeplechaser to jump and conveyed to his official, very high-powered trainer my anxiety that the horse had a rather pottering, unlevel trot. His response was to pat me on the shoulder and say, 'You don't win races in trot, my dear.' I was duly humbled, especially as the horse went on to win many good steeplechases.

The trot must be rhythmical, balanced and active, but you must be careful to ride it within the horse's ability to balance. It is no good powering along trying to make him active when in fact you are riding him out of balance. Every horse has a tempo and rhythm which suits him, and you can ask for activity within this, but do not power too much. On the other hand, many horses find it easier to slop along without sufficient activity, and this is where your helper on the ground must advise you. Activity must be achieved by asking the horse to use his hocks and step forward under his body into a steady rein contact.

A lower outline enables a novice horse to use the muscles over the top line of his body. As he strengthens and progresses, his weight is transferred further back and his forehand becomes lighter and lighter. It is normally better to ride the novice horse in rising trot, especially if you yourself are not very supple in sitting trot. Later on, however, you must work on your balance and suppleness in order to be able to perform sitting trot, which gives far greater control once you have mastered the art.

In novice tests the work is done in *working trot*. This is a workmanlike, active but not hurried trot showing a balanced, rhythmical pace. The horse should track up: i.e. the footfalls of his hind feet should step forward into the prints left by his forefeet. In early Novice tests you may be asked to show some lengthened strides – this is working towards medium trot, where you ask for more impulsion but maintain the rhythm. The strides should start to lengthen but not hurry and the horse should lengthen the top line of his body.

24. The trot: two-time sequence.

25. Extended trot.

(b)   (b)

Medium trot is a continuation of this lengthening, so the horse maintains a consistent lengthening of stride and frame for the required distance. At a higher level, as in the walk, you will be required to show *extended trot*. The horse must then show as much lengthening of stride as possible while maintaining his balance throughout.

In *collected trot*, as in collected walk, the steps become shorter, the horse's hind legs step further under his body and his centre of gravity shifts further back, enabling him to raise his forehand and lighten in front. He must not collect by simply slowing down – the energy must still be there. As with collected walk, collected trot is very useful in training although it is not used in FEI tests

The canter

This is a crucial pace for a jumping horse. It is a three-time pace from which most jumping is done, and if the horse has a naturally balanced, good canter it makes approaching fences so much simpler. A horse with good, round steps is normally easier than long, daisy-cutting steps.

To train the canter for jumping, you need to be able to lengthen and shorten the stride. The novice tests include *working canter* but further up the scale you will need to do *medium canter*, *extended canter* and *collected canter*. This means being able to make the strides both longer and shorter while remembering to maintain the balance, rhythm and impulsion throughout.

26. *The canter: three-time sequence.*

Rein-back

Rein-back is a difficult movement to teach the horse at first, but once he understands he should not have a problem. Initially you can stand on the ground and, with one hand on his head and the other on his shoulder, push him back a couple of steps and say, 'whoah, back'. This helps a young horse to understand. When mounted it is vital that you do not pull him back – if you do he will learn to shorten his neck, put his chin in his chest and become restricted, which reduces his ability to move freely.

Ride him to a good, square halt, then draw your lower legs slightly back and close them to give a forward aid. You then close your hand on the rein to prevent him stepping forwards, and he will learn that you want him to step backwards. You must also lighten your seat, as in order to step back he will slightly raise his back but must not raise his head.

Lateral work

Both horse and rider will learn a lot about control, suppleness and direction by starting some lateral work. This can be fairly simple. Start by teaching the horse such movements as *turn on the forehand*, which encourages him to move from a leg aid and to step sideways, and *leg yielding*, in which the horse moves forwards and sideways away from the leg. For this you must have control of the horse through both your legs – i.e. if leg yielding to the right, the horse moves forwards and sideways, maintaining a straight body with a slight flexion to the left. However, although your left leg asks the horse to move sideways, your right leg must be still and on the girth to keep the forward movement in the horse and to prevent him falling too sharply sideways.

(c)

In the more advanced tests you will need to learn:

(a) Counter canter
(b) Shoulder-in
(c) Travers
(d) Half-pass
(e) Flying changes

(a) *Counter canter* is an exercise to improve the balance and suppleness of your horse. It involves changing the rein and being able to maintain the leading leg. Provided you keep the correct bend towards the leading leg with slight flexion at the poll, and sit in balance, maintaining the aids as in true canter, your horse will be able to fulfil this task. However, if you change the aids or make any sudden changes in your weight distribution, the horse is likely to change legs in order to keep his balance. This movement often starts with a simple half-circle, returning and continuing down the arena and then proceeding around the short end of the arena, or even riding a serpentine.

(b) *Shoulder-in* can be introduced once your horse has a good understanding of going forward straight and balanced, and once you are fully aware of what your leg, rein and weight aids are for. It is important for the rhythm to be maintained and for the angle not to be too extreme. It can be practised in walk as long as the horse remains forward-thinking, then in trot once he understands the aids. The horse should be on three tracks with a slight bend throughout his body round the inside leg.

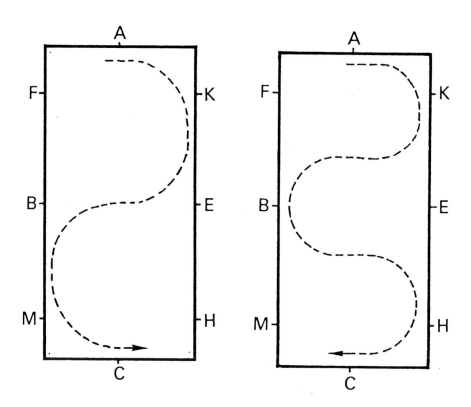

Left 27. *Two half-circles.*   Right 28. *Three-loop serpentine.*

Shoulder-in ridden incorrectly will often show only a neck bend in the horse or too steep an angle, which results in leg yielding. You must remain over the horse's centre of gravity and turn your body in line with his.

(c) *Travers* is a movement used in preparation for half-pass. This asks the horse to be supple behind the saddle and to bring his hind quarters on to an inner track while maintaining straightness in the shoulder, head and neck.

(d) In *half-pass*, the horse moves forward and sideways with a bend in the direction in which he is going. Again, the rhythm, impulsion and balance must be maintained as in shoulder-in, with the bend round the inside leg. The forehand should be slightly in advance of the quarters. The rider must look ahead and keep the correct angle throughout. This movement will be done on both reins, to show up any stiffness on either side, so it is important that you make your horse supple on both reins.

(e) *Flying changes* involve changing from one leading leg to the other

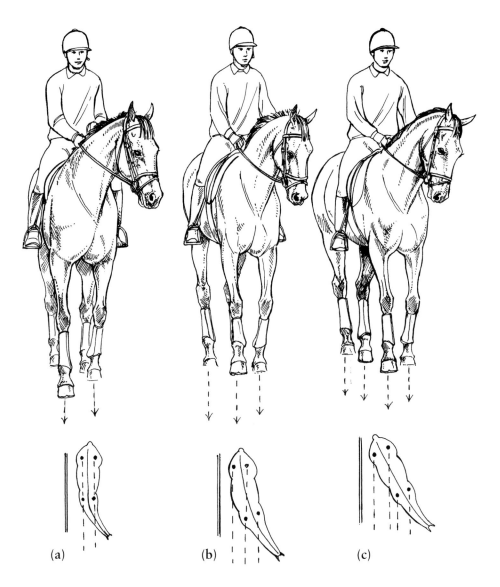

29. *Shoulder-in: (a) on two tracks with insufficient body angle and too much bend in neck; (b) correct, on three tracks; (c) incorrect, on four tracks.*

without going through trot. They are very useful in all jump training, and if taught early will be a great asset. They also feature in more advanced dressage tests. Many horses effect them naturally when jumping, which is a great asset as it enables them to be balanced when turning and changing direction. However, they may find them more difficult to perform when asked to do so on the flat. In the early stages of training a change of rein is generally involved.

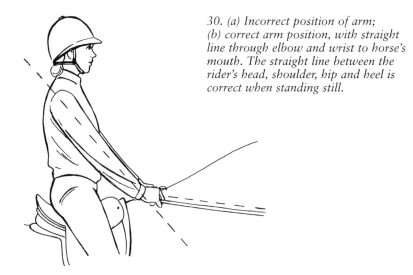

30. (a) Incorrect position of arm; (b) correct arm position, with straight line through elbow and wrist to horse's mouth. The straight line between the rider's head, shoulder, hip and heel is correct when standing still.

(a)

(b)

When there is more than one judge they will not all have the same view of these movements because they will see them from different angles, so individual marks may vary. However, each judge can detect if the rhythm or balance are lost. Judges are generally positioned, in separate vehicles or cubicles, at the short end of the arena opposite the entry point. Having more than one judge allows for a better assessment of the horse's strengths, especially in transitions.

Ringcraft – how to approach the test

First, know your test thoroughly. In horse trials you cannot have it read out, and there is nothing worse than forgetting it half-way through. If possible, watch someone ride it and see how it should be performed, or learn by their mistakes. Watch as if you were the judge and suddenly you will see how easy it is to make unnecessary errors.

Arrive in plenty of time. You will have been given your starting time beforehand, so plan your riding-in accordingly. At least 30 minutes before your allotted time, check with the steward that everything is running to time. Before you enter the arena the steward will check your tack, but it is your responsibility to make sure that everything is correct. When you ride around the outside of the arena and are given the signal to start, you have only one minute (45 seconds under FEI rules) before you **must** enter the arena.

Working-in

How you work-in is important. You do not want your horse too fresh; on the other hand he needs a little sparkle to show off in the test. It is often a good idea to work-in by hacking around and letting him take in the surroundings before settling down to more serious work. If he is exceptionally cheeky it may be wise to ride him twice – use the first time to settle him, then prepare yourself while he relaxes in the horsebox and bring him out again with a little time to ride in before the test.

Lungeing is another possibility, but may not be allowed due to lack of space and should only be carried out by someone experienced. Side reins are only permissable under Pony Club rules. The value of good lungeing is that it prevents horse and rider from transmitting their nerves or agitation to each other.

It is not suitable for a novice to lunge a horse in a strange environment, as he may escape and be a danger to himself and anyone else in his way. Learn to lunge in an enclosed area with an expert, and only venture forth at a competition when you are experienced and aware of your horse's temperament.

31. Good novice outline, although hock is trailing slightly.

32. Incorrect outline: neck shortened, hock trailing.

What the judge is looking for

At novice levels the judge is looking for a well-trained horse who is progressing along the right lines, so there is no need to try to 'pull the horse together' and destroy his balance. Four factors are necessary to gain good marks:

- Straightness
- Rhythm
- Impulsion
- Accuracy

Of course, the training leading up to the test will prepare the horse for the movements required and for the suppleness and activity that he needs.

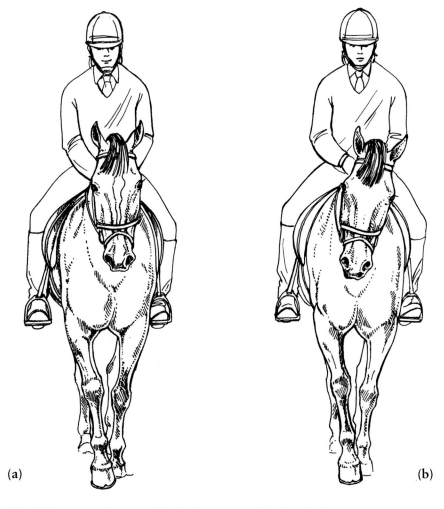

(a)   (b)

33. (a) Correct outline: straight. (b) Incorrect outline: head tilting.

Learn movements individually, and only ride the whole test when you are familiar with each movement and have perfected it. When riding-in, the most important factor is to relax the horse in order to allow him to go in a basically correct outline from leg to rein, working from behind.

Straightness is apparent at the very start. If you come down the centre line wobbling from side to side, the judge does not receive a favourable impression. The horse must not only remain on the straight line, but his head and neck must not be tilting either way.

Circles are often ridden egg-shaped. Draw a circle and study it. Mark one out in your arena at home and practise riding round it.

Accuracy is important. Prepare in advance, so that transitions are ridden exactly at the markers.

Marks

Each test is divided into numbered blocks, with a maximum mark of 10 to be awarded in each. In FEI events there is a standard scoring system. All dressage tests are marked out of 250. The judge's mark is then subtracted from 250, so, for example, 175 good marks equals 75 penalties.

Under national rules, in dressage the good marks are added together, subtracted from the total available and the remaining figure equals the penalty marks. In order to keep the correct influence of dressage to show jumping to cross-country, a co-efficient of 2/5 is then applied to the mark to give the final dressage penalty score. This may eventually change to be in line with FEI rules.

As well as the marks for each movement, at the end of the test sheet there are four collective marks (these may be x2) for:

(a) Paces
(b) Impulsion
(c) Submission
(d) Rider

(a) *Paces*. A horse with good natural paces has an advantage here, but of course having good paces and showing them off correctly in a test are two different things!

(b) *Impulsion* is the desire to move forward; elasticity of steps; and engagement of the hind-quarters. It is important for the horse to be active, but this must not be confused with speed. Impulsion is vital in all the disciplines.

(c) *Submission* is attention and obedience; lightness and ease of movements; and acceptance of the bridle. This mark shows up any tension, lack of suppleness or unwillingness to go forward from leg to rein.

(d) *Rider*. Position, seat and correct use of the aids. This is the judge's opinion of the skills of the rider.

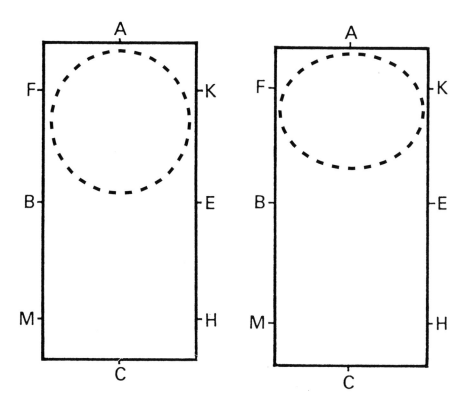

Left *34. Diagram showing good circle.*   Right *35. Poor, egg-shaped circle.*

Remember:

- When you learn the test, take note of how many movements comprise one block. Sometimes you will find that a single 20-metre circle can gain a whole 10 marks, which underlines the importance of accuracy and thinking ahead.
- If a movement is required to start at a particular letter, it is the rider's shoulder on passing the marker (or halting opposite it) that the judge is looking for. For example, if you halt at C your shoulder should be level with the marker.
- If a movement goes badly, focus on the next one. You cannot do anything about the error, so press on and make sure that it does not affect your concentration.
- If you lose your way, the judge will stop you by sounding a bell, whistle, car horn or whatever, and will advise you as to how to correct your course. Don't panic, just take a deep breath and try not to fluster your horse. If you rectify the mistake before the judge stops you, such as rising or sitting in a trot movement, you will be allowed to continue but will forfeit two penalties on your final score.

Show Jumping

Event horses tend to be enthusiastic and forward-thinking and to have the cross-country in their minds, so they often go too fast and jump carelessly. An event horse needs to acquire a good technique at an early age while maintaining his athletic ability. The rider, too, must acquire plenty of experience in this phase.

Every event has a different show jumping course, which you must walk before the class begins so that you can ride it confidently and positively.

Producing a fluent, balanced round in the show jumping requires the same basic training skills as for a good dressage test. As well as being able to jump, the horse must be controlled, balanced and obedient to the aids, so that he can negotiate turns and changes of direction and lengthen and shorten his stride on command. Horse and rider must also have complete confidence in each other.

In eventing, the aim of the show jumping phase is to show the horse's ability to jump correctly and carefully rather than especially high. Courses are designed to encourage obedience, balance and control, which can sometimes be difficult on a fit eventer.

- Do be careful not to confuse speed with impulsion. To complete a show-jumping round carefully you need to maintain an active, controlled canter stride and good balance in the horse.
- Create a forward, positive canter.
- Be alert and remember to look and think ahead.
- Do make sure that you know your way.
- Don't be caught asleep coming to the first fence.

The course will consist of eight to 10 fences, varying from uprights to spreads with heights and widths according to the level of the class. Most course builders try to make the first fence an inviting one, usually an ascending spread. They will also include some *related distances*, where one fence is built a planned distance from the next to test the rider's ability to recognise it when walking the course and then the ability to maintain, shorten and lengthen the canter accordingly.

Most related distances are three, four or five strides. A short-striding horse might put in extra strides, or an unruly horse might cancel out strides, but the important thing to remember is that in order to jump cleanly and safely the horse must be controlled, balanced and in front of the leg, so that the rider can then choose to lengthen or shorten the stride.

Each course will contain a *double*, with a distance of one or two strides between the two fences. Careful walking is essential. At higher levels a *treble* (three obstacles with one or two strides between each) will be included.

The time allowed for a novice course is comfortable so if you keep up a good rhythm you should not incur time faults. However, as you advance up the levels the time becomes a little quicker and it is easy to collect a time fault, which can mean the difference between winning and coming second.

Practice fences

Before you start, have a few jumps over the practice fences supplied. There are usually two or three: one cross-pole, one upright and one oxer, which you can adjust to your own liking. However, the wings will be taped to show the maximum height to which you are allowed to build the fence. Do check the rules as to what type of fence you are allowed to build in the practice arena, as to disobey can mean elimination before you've even started. The fences will be flagged red and white and you must only jump them in one direction, with the red flag on your right. Check that the going does not become too deep; if it does, move the fence.

36. *Practice show jump.*

Do not over-jump your horse over the practice fences. Remember that you want to loosen him up and get your eye in, as well as his, but to save his best jumping for the competition arena. This especially applies to a three-day event, when the horse may well be tired on the last day and, although he will need to be loosened up, he must not be overworked.

Scoring

Penalties for errors according to Pony Club and BHTA rules are as follows:

Knockdown	5 penalties
1st refusal	10
2nd refusal	20
3rd refusal	elimination
Fall of horse or rider	30
2nd fall	elimination
Error of course not rectified	elimination
Retaking obstacle already jumped	elimination
Jumping obstacle in wrong order	elimination
Starting before bell	elimination
Not going between start/finish markers	elimination

Time penalties are as stated in the Rule Book.

Other important rules

• After the starting bell has rung you have 30 seconds (45 under FEI rules) to start and can be eliminated if you take longer.
• You must not cross your tracks when approaching a fence, particularly after a refusal.
• If your horse refuses, you must not show him the fence.
• Your whip should not be more than 76cm (30in) long.

Walking the show-jumping course

This is a really important part of the job. Be aware of the route, the type of going and the position of the collecting ring in relation to the arena, as many young horses tend to hang towards it. Check where the start and finish are, as when you pass between them you trigger the timing equipment. Failure to do so means elimination, and they can be surprisingly easy to miss. Take note of any related distances (*see page 60*) and be aware of whether your horse is long- or short-striding, as this will affect how you ride them.

An average length of a show jumping canter stride is approximately 3.5m (12ft). Normally the elements of a one-stride double will be set at a distance of 8m (24-27ft) apart. To walk a distance, pace from the centre of the back pole of one fence to the centre of the front pole of the next.

Two-stride double	11m (36ft)
Three-stride related distance	14m (45-48ft)
Four-stride related distance	18m (58-60ft)

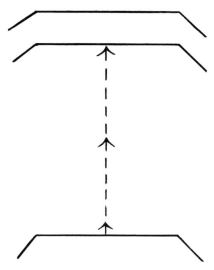

37. Walking the distance between two fences.

You will generally land about 6ft from a fence and take off 6ft from the next one, though how close or far out a horse will actually jump will be determined by the type of fence. From an upright and a parallel he will take off and land at similar distances. Over an ascending spread such as a triple bar he is likely to land further out, as the highest point of his jump will be over the back rail. You must take this into account when walking a related distance after a triple bar or ascending spread.

When you walk the course, be aware of sharp turns and sloping ground, as these can easily upset your balance and rhythm. Horses will often speed up downhill and lose impulsion uphill, so you must be ready to counteract this.

Important training points for the jumping phases
1. The rider must establish a good balance on the horse. You must have a secure lower leg position, and this takes a lot of practice. Once your lower leg position is established, with your weight on your feet, you have far more freedom of movement in the rest of your body. If you grip with your knees it is very difficult to keep your lower legs in close contact with the horse to maintain impulsion.

38. A good, balanced position for a rider preparing to jump, with a light seat, weight on to foot and the angle between ankle, knee and hip joints more acute than for dressage so that they act as shock absorbers. The lower leg is a good base, with a straight line from knee to toe.

2. The rider must be looking ahead, as this is a great help in turning the horse, and is thus vital to the smooth riding of a course.

3. Establishing a good canter enables the horse to make the most of his ability. In fact, you need to spend more time working on the canter than actually jumping. The canter must be going forward *in balance*, with a good *rhythm*; these are words you will hear a lot, but they are so important. You need to be able to increase and decrease the pace without losing impulsion, and this requires more activity from the horse's hind legs. A common fault when the rider wishes to shorten the stride is to use too much rein and not enough leg, so the horse falls into a trot.

Remember to sit still and allow him to jump the fence. Rein contact is important to maintain control but the horse needs some movement of his head and neck for balance and focus of vision. If you have a *forward, positive, balanced* canter you have made the task easier for your horse.

The Cross-Country

Riding the cross-country phase should be enjoyable and safe. Itis vital for the horse always to maintain his enthusiasm and his soundness – both essential components of success.

Familiarity with various types of terrain and ground, such as hilly, sandy, stony, soft and hard going, are all critical factors in the final result. A judgment of pace and how best to conserve a horse's energy is a skill that needs endless practice. **It is far better to acquire time faults initially than to push your horse too hard. Only when he has good control and balance is it safe to go faster.** A confident horse is one who is given a thoughtful progression through the different levels.

Building a partnership with your horse so that you can trust one another and be confident across country means plenty of time spent perfecting simple, basic tasks. Get a young horse used to all types of going underfoot by hacking through woods, where he needs to look where he puts his feet, up and down hills, through puddles and streams, up and down banks and so on. All this will teach him self-preservation. Hunting soon teaches a young horse to look where he is going and be confident in all situations. Following an older horse is also an excellent way in which to teach your horse new lessons.

In the cross-country phase of an event there is a set time allowed for the course, which is decided according to the speed required for the particular level (*see appendix A*). At the time of writing, pre-novice classes are run at 490 metres per minute and novice classes at 520 mpm, but do check the rules.

With a novice horse it is not advisable to make the speed your priority. Introduce him purposefully to the challenge, remembering that both horse and rider must be positive and attacking in attitude but must not rely on speed to get over the fences. The more confident and experienced you both become, the faster you can safely go – but watch the top class riders and you will see that they always ride into cross-country fences with those two crucial factors, control and balance.

The secret of accurate timing is walking the course, seeing the most direct routes between fences and not pushing your horse out of rhythm so that you end up hauling at the reins in an attempt to achieve some control for the fences.

Refusals can happen for several reasons:
(a) The approach was incorrect:
> *Too fast*. The horse has no time to see what he has to do.
> *Not enough impulsion*. This is less likely, except in cases where the
> horse is approaching a fence without control, is still being steadied by

the rider, and is therefore unable to go forward to the fence.

Not straight – the horse has insufficient time to see the obstacle. The approach is vital when you are jumping fences at an angle.

(b) The fence is too difficult for the horse's level of education.

(c) The horse is not bold by nature and is not enjoying the task.

(d) The rider is not naturally bold and is not enjoying the task.

The penalties in a one-day event are designed to give you a fair chance of completing the course, but also to stop you pressing on when the horse has had enough. You can find full details in your rule book, but the basic BHTA system is as follows:

1st refusal	20 penalties (40 under FEI rules)
2nd refusal at same fence	40 pen (80 under FEI rules)
3rd refusal at same fence	elimination
fall of horse or rider	60 pen (120 under FEI rules)
2nd fall	elimination

Time faults are in the rule book. Remember: you can incur penalties for going too fast as well as too slow.

Walking the course

This is a vital part of the cross-country phase. If you are not very experienced, plan to walk the course at least twice, once preferably with a knowledgeable adviser. Use your first walk to give you a general impression of the fences and the ground – whether it is flat or hilly, stony or smooth, slippery, wet or boggy. Try to see the course with an alert, fresh concentration, as this is how your horse will see it. Make a mental image of the fences and terrain, so that just before setting off you can picture every turn, fence and type of going.

With your adviser, choose your route between fences, and when obstacles have alternatives, decide which way will be best for you and your horse. Look back to the previous fence to see if you walked a straight line, and note whether you need to make a detour round a bad patch of ground or to get a better approach. The quickest route is not always the best, and there is nothing heroic about taking it. Choosing the less difficult alternative may be better in the long run as novice horses, as well as novice riders, need to be introduced to different fences gradually in order to gain confidence in their own ability.

Walking the course with someone more experienced means that they can point out pitfalls before you have a chance to fall into them. It is a good idea to do the second walk alone, walking round positively without too much hesitation. Looking for a landmark in the distance, such as a

39. You can learn at all ages: the author giving advice in Chantilly.

tree, can help you plan a line. Note the state of the going, which will determine whether or not your horse needs studs in his shoes.

When the going is deep it is more tiring for the horse, so where possible look for the best ground for take-off and landing. Once you are riding the course you can use your intelligence and avoid tracks made by other horses.

It is essential to walk the alternative routes since if you have a late start time, you may have to adjust your plans to suit the going. Jumping out of deep going not only makes the fence considerably higher but also causes more chance of injuries from strain, loss of shoes or over-reaching.

Some obstacles you might meet

During training you will have learned how to approach different types of fence, so bear this in mind on your course-walk. If you know the correct pace at which to tackle different obstacles, you will arrive at the jump with the horse well balanced and able to cope. Too fast too soon is a passport to trouble later on.

The fences fall into several categories requiring different tactics:

40. *Ditch in front.*

41. *Inviting brush-type fence with ditch behind.*

42. *Angled rails over ditch.*

43. *Bank and rails off.*

44. *Rails without a direct approach.*

45. *Step up to rail.*

46. *Into water before keyhole.*

47. *Keyhole.*

48. *Nice rounded log-type fence and ditch.*

49. Water complex.

Straightforward fences with brush on top can be approached with greater speed and a stronger pace, provided the horse is IN BALANCE. *Do not* prepare your horse way out and drive him forward, as this often puts him out of balance. Instead, wait for the fence to come to you, so that as you get closer you can allow the horse to focus and make his decisions, and back this up with your leg. The degree of leg required will depend on his reaction to the fence.

Bullfinches. These are fences with a thin but very high brush which the horse has to jump through. They need practice, as some horses feel they must clear the whole height of the fence.

Obstacles with a ditch in front have the advantage of giving the horse a good ground line to stand off the fence, but beware that he does not back off slightly. Be ready with your leg.

Drop fences require a balanced, forward approach, with the rider more upright. It is generally better for the horse to jump out over the drop rather than land too steeply and unbalanced. Make sure that your stride is not too long as this, too, will unbalance the landing.

50. *Bullfinch.*

Obstacles with a ditch between two fences (formerly known as 'coffins') require a shortened stride. Sit up and be careful not to get ahead of the horse, as if he suddenly sees the ditch he is more likely to stop at the first element.

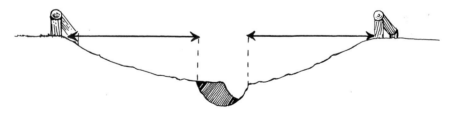

51. *Ditch between two fences: correct line of jumping.*

Landing over a drop on sloping ground is not as jarring as landing over a drop on flat ground. Sliding the reins – that is, letting the reins lengthen so that the horse can use his neck – is a useful skill to learn as it makes it easier for the horse to balance. But you must stay over his centre of gravity throughout, so practise re-taking the rein contact and riding him forward from leg to rein on landing.

Combination fences, including bounces, need a controlled, shortened stride, but make sure that you allow the stride to be forward and short rather than just holding it. The hind leg must be allowed to come more underneath the horse so that he can raise his forehand without being restricted by the rein contact. Practise bounces over show jump poles with wings so that you can alter the size as you gain expertise.

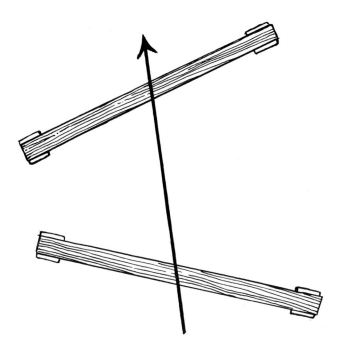

52. Angled rails: walk the distance to find the correct line for your horse.

Arrowheads and angled rails show up the increasing need for precision and accuracy in cross-country riding. You need to be able to alter the pace from a cross-country gallop to a short, controlled canter smoothly and with relative ease. This really shows up the obedience of the horse.

Corners. It is best to practise these at home with a show jump and a plastic drum, starting small and increasing the size when you have achieved accuracy. Straightness is the key, which again comes down to the flat work. Horses drifting in one direction or other can sway a rider's decision as to whether it is wise to take the direct route. The object of jumping a corner is to bisect a line through the centre, taking the angle that is 90 degrees to the centre rail. Finding the wrong line, as shown in the diagram, is really asking for big trouble!

Psychologically it can be good to imagine that you are jumping a narrow parallel. Doubles of corners, which you would meet at intermediate level and above, need a similar approach, with positive direction from the rider. A negative attitude will lead to a 'glance-off': i.e. a run-out and faults. The technique mentioned in the course-walking section of this chapter, of picking a distant point such as a tree or telegraph pole to aim for, is very useful with corner fences.

Jumping from light to dark can pose a problem, with the horse not adjusting to the fence in time – so beware of going too fast.

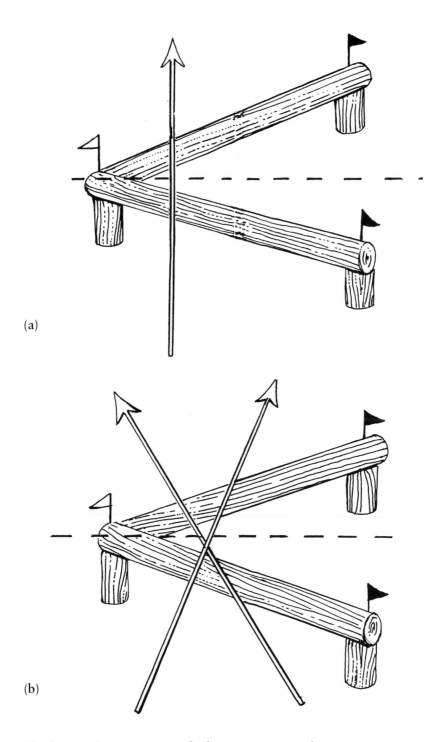

(a)

(b)

53. Corners: (a) correct approach, (b) incorrect approaches.

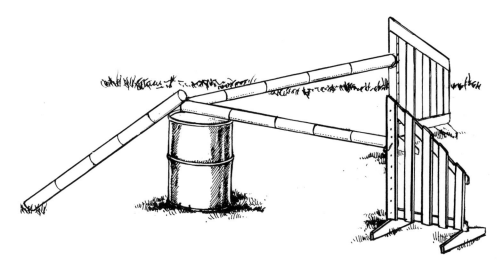

54. *Home-made practice corner.*

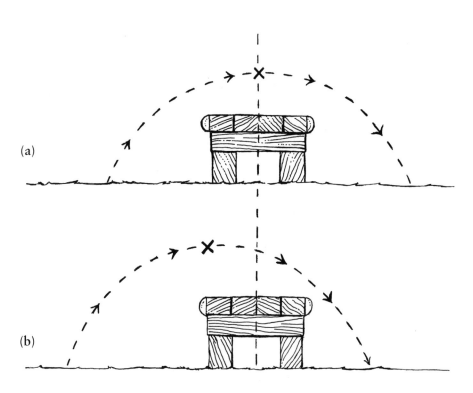

(a)

(b)

55. *Correct (a) and incorrect (b) ways of jumping an oxer.*

Stirrup length for cross-country and steeplechase

As a guide, your stirrups should be shorter than for show jumping. It is important to close the angles between ankle, knee and hip to maintain a balanced position at a faster pace.

Your lower leg is the security anchor, and your ankle joint must be flexible in order to keep your weight firmly on your foot. If the stirrups are too long, you may end up resting all your weight on the horse's back; if they are too short you will feel insecure and could well get jumped out of the saddle.

Practice with short stirrups is vital to gain strength and improve balance. Your knees need to be flexible and act as springs, but it's all too easy to stand without flexing your joints. A good exercise is to go into jumping position in trot, weight out of the saddle, putting pressure through the ball of your foot and into your heel. You can use the horse's neck forsupport at first so that you do not rely on his mouth. Try to maintain this position for two minutes to begin with, then build it up to six or seven minutes, eventually without needing to use the horse's neck.

In the steeplechase, the length of your stirrups again depends on personal preference – the shorter the better – but the most important factor is to be able to adopt a lower leg position that is a little further forward. If you should make a mistake you will be able to keep 'in the plate'. Loss of control often occurs when the rider loses his or her balance and starts to pull against the horse. All too often the remedy resorted to is changing to a stronger bit, when perhaps the rider really needs to be more aware of his or her own position and balance.

Working-in

You need to work your horse in before the cross-country, but at a one-day event you will most likely have done both dressage and show jumping beforehand, so all you need to do is adjust your stirrups to cross-country length and jump one or two fences to make sure you feel comfortable. This is more for your own sake than the horse's.

One-day events are often run over two days if there are a lot of entries, in which case you might have to do dressage on day one and show jumping and cross-country on day two. If this happens, remember to arrive with plenty of time to work your horse in on day two. Loosening up and preparing for a competition is as important for a horse as it is for a gymnast or any other athlete.

You will have been given a start time, which you must keep to unless otherwise instructed, so plan your warm-up accordingly. Do check in

56. The ultimate aim: 'going for it' at Badminton. This photograph was taken in the pouring rain in 1999.

advance with the collecting ring steward in case there has been a delay. If the competition is running ahead of itself you are allowed to wait for your allotted time, but it is always better to help the organisers by going when they are ready for you.

Your stirrups may feel rather short as you wait at the start but don't worry: once you are in a forward position and jumping fences you will soon feel much more comfortable. If the stirrups are too long your legs will not provide a good base, and to make yourself feel secure you will probably end up taking your weight on the saddle and becoming a dead weight on your horse's back.

In the start box, the count-down is usually from 5. It is important to stay as calm as possible so that you get the best possible start.

6

Travelling

Any journey is better for being well planned, as it can be a stressful time for both horse and rider. Some tips to remember are:
• Always keep your vehicle well serviced. Breaking down is bad enough in a car, but with horses it poses a whole host of problems
• Travel with another person, so that there is someone to help if you break down.
• Work out your route in advance
• Allow plenty of time for the journey. It is much better to arrive in time for a cup of coffee than to be tearing around in a panic.

Most horses travel well in modern trailers and horseboxes but there are exceptions, and you should be aware of this when you buy a horse. Decide how he travels best – for example, some horses find it hard to balance in a narrow space as they cannot spread their feet wide enough, so they lean on the partition and lose their footing. This is alarming and once it has happened the best solution is to widen the area or remove the partition, as no amount of scolding the horse will improve the situation – it will only frighten him more.

Some horses travel better facing forwards, some backwards, and some herringbone. Although you cannot constantly change your mode of transport, try to ensure that the horse is comfortable because if the journey is a long one it may well affect his performance. Make sure that there is good ventilation – fresh air is vital on journeys of any length.

Feeding needs careful thought. It is good to keep to as normal a routine as possible, bearing in mind the length of the journey and the task at the other end. For example, do not give him a large haynet en route to an event if you have an early cross-country time. Although he must not eat excessively before competing, you must not starve him for hours beforehand or his digestive system will stop working efficiently and he may end up with colic. Water is also important and should either be available at all

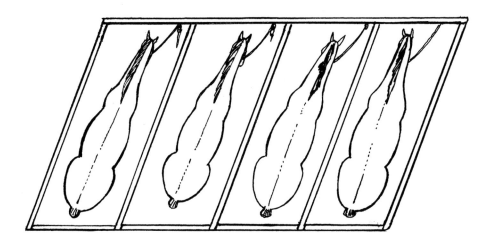

57. Diagram showing herringbone method of transporting horses.

times en route or offered regularly on a long journey, especially in hot conditions.

Many boxes have rubber flooring, which is very practical, but wood-shavings or equivalent, spread on top, will make it more comfortable for the horse. On a long journey, regular mucking out will make the atmosphere more pleasant and will ensure that it does not affect the horse's breathing. When you clean the horsebox out after the journey, remember to remove matting and to check the floorboards underneath, as they can rot. At a competition, **do not muck out your horsebox into someone** else's **field** – find a muck heap.

Transporting horses by air and sea is not complicated if you follow the same rules as for road travel, but on long sea and land journeys you will need to arrange places to stop overnight so that the horses have satisfactory stabling and rest. Ten hours is long enough for one move. For foreign trips it is advisable to use a horse transport agency, as they have all the relevant knowledge and experience.

Always drive with the horses in mind. Remember: *they* have no choice.

Arrival

When you arrive at an event, make sure that you have enough time for the horse to settle and for you to prepare without having to panic. There is always plenty to do – collecting numbers, checking everything is running to time, walking courses, tacking up, possibly putting studs in, and changing your own clothes or even having a snack.

Clothing for travel

Rugs for travel must be appropriate to the weather and to the number of horses in the horsebox. Check them regularly on a long journey and make any necessary changes.

For legs, wool bandages over Gamgee or Fibregee give good protection, but they must be applied correctly. Bandages that are too tight can cause serious injury to tendons.

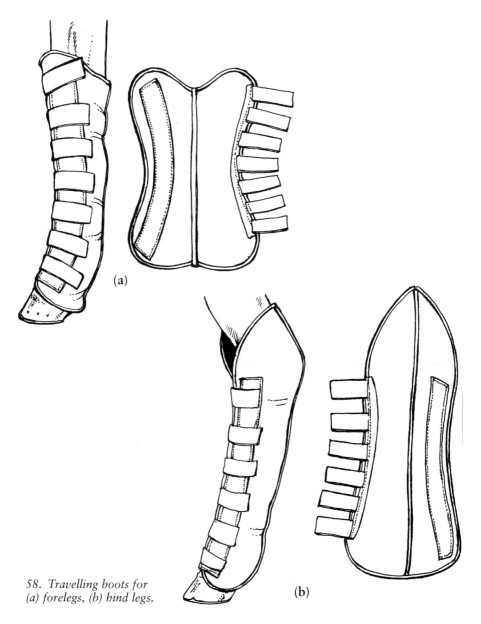

(a)

(b)

58. *Travelling boots for (a) forelegs, (b) hind legs.*

59. Horse ready for travelling.

Likewise, tail bandages are fine for short trips, but to stay in place for a long journey they are often put on too tight and can then rub and cause bad sores on the dock. A well-fitting tail guard may be more suitable.

Travelling boots are very useful and efficient. They must be fastened securely, preferably with Velcro, so that they do not slip. They are designed to offer protection low down over the coronet, as well as to knee and hock, thus saving you from having to use extra knee and hock boots.

60. Rider and horse ready for dressage.

7

Equipment for Competitions

Dressage

THE HORSE
Saddle When you are starting out, a general purpose (GP) saddle is fine for all the disciplines. A GP is not straight-cut or deep-seated like a dressage saddle, nor is it as forward-cut as a jumping saddle. Later, when you know you're going to continue, a dressage saddle can be useful – but beware of being sold one that's very deep and pre-determines your position. Whichever saddle you use, do have it professionally fitted because a badly-fitting saddle, however comfortable it is for you, can do lasting damage to the horse. Too narrow and it will pinch the withers; too wide and it will press on them; and the seat must distribute your weight evenly on the horse's back.

Bridle In novice tests you have to use a snaffle bridle with a noseband. Various types of snaffle are allowed, as are various nosebands – you can find details in the rule book, along with a list of any other tack allowed and how it changes as you move up the levels. Martingales are not allowed.

Boots Not allowed.

THE RIDER
(See the Pony Club publication *Correct Dress for Riders*.)
At Pony Club and pony trials you may wear jodhpurs and jodhpur boots, a shirt and tie, and jacket. At senior level you will need breeches (beige or buff) and long boots, tie or stock, and jacket. At novice level a tweed jacket is fine, but as you progress a dark jacket (black or navy) and a white stock become necessary. Once you reach advanced, a top hat and tail coat are allowed but not essential, although riders often choose to wear them

for elegance. A hat of the correct standard is required. (Be sure to check the current rule book.)At the time of writing a chin strap is not essential, but always check the rule book in case this changes. Gloves are essential. Spurs are not essential until advanced level, except for all FEI tests.

Show Jumping

THE HORSE

Saddle Your GP saddle is fine but as you get more serious you may prefer a longer-seated, more forward-cut jumping saddle.

61. Rider and horse ready for show jumping.

Bridle The choice of bits and nosebands is wider, and standing, Irish and running martingales are all allowed in Pony Club competitions. Standing martingales are not allowed in BHTA events.

Boots The horse can wear leg protection, though he may not need too much. See the cross-country section for more details, then decide what you need for show jumping.

THE RIDER
Your hat must be a crash hat of the correct standard, with a navy or black cover, and the chin strap must be fastened at all times when you are on the horse. Spurs are optional. Whips are optional but should not exceed 76cm (30in). Gloves are optional, as are body protectors of the correct standard (see rule book).

Cross-Country

THE HORSE
Saddle You need space to pull up your stirrups and slide your seat back.

Rawhide stirrup leathers are toughest, therefore safest, and stainless steel stirrup irons are stronger than nickel ones. Stirrup treads are vital, as they stop your feet slipping out.

Girths can be leather or webbing. Some have an elastic inset, but if you use one of these take care not to over-tighten it, as this would put a lot of pressure on the horse's belly and make it sore.

Bridle The same rules are applicable as for show jumping. Use non-slip reins. Rubber-covered ones are easiest to hold, but some riders prefer continental reins, which are webbing with leather strips.

Do check all your tack regularly. Stitching can rot, and general wear and tear can cause breaks. The areas most likely to deteriorate are the stitching on stirrup leathers, girths and reins. Check bits for wear and for roughness.

Boots There are so many different types of leg protection available that it's difficult to decide what your horse really needs. Remember that he is an athlete, so too much weight on his legs can hinder rather than enhance his performance. In racing there is a saying that goes, 'An ounce on the leg is equal to a pound in the saddle'.

Inevitably there will be occasions when a horse will inflict injuries on one limb or another. There are many types of protective boot available,

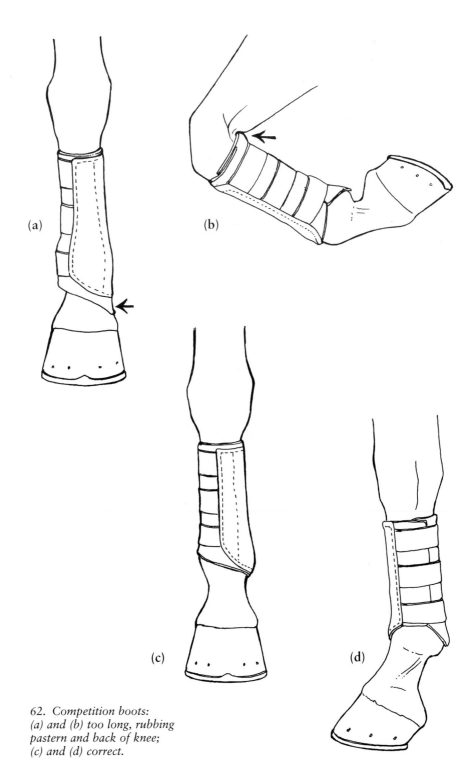

62. Competition boots:
(a) and (b) too long, rubbing
pastern and back of knee;
(c) and (d) correct.

some of which do more harm than good. What you use will always be a compromise. Remember that in action the shape of the horse's leg is constantly changing, so you need a flexible boot. However flexible the boot seems, if it constricts the leg it will restrict the blood supply, so any stretchy material must not have a strong recoil, otherwise damage will occur after a surprisingly short time.

Examples of good boots:
1 Neoprene secured by multiple Velcro fasteners.
Advantages
• Light
• Don't hold water
• Easy to clean
• Flexible
• Conform to changing leg shapes
• Rarely cause pressure sores
• Good boot if correct size (too long may rub pastern, too high may cut into back of knee when leg is flexed).
Disadvantages
• Will not protect from laceration or impact.

2 Leather with Neoprene lining.
Especially good with multiple straps and buckles, though they are more expensive. Most of the above advantages apply but these boots offer even more protection. They can be thoroughly soaked when new and thus adapted to fit a particular horse. The leather must always be kept flexible.

Examples of bad boots
1 Boots with inflexible, rigid inserts. These need careful fitting because though they may appear to fit when a horse is standing still they can easily restrict movement and cause pressure sores.
2 Boots with powerful elastic recoil, which will interfere with circulation and cause damage.
3 Any boots with lining that changes with water saturation, such as fleece, will not be suitable for cross-country.

Over-reach boots These can be useful, but care must be taken to ensure that they fit correctly. If they are too large, the horse can easily tread on one, and trip. If they are too tight, rubbing can occur around the pastern. Also, it is advisable not to leave them on too long, as they can cause chafing, especially during hot weather or in sandy going.

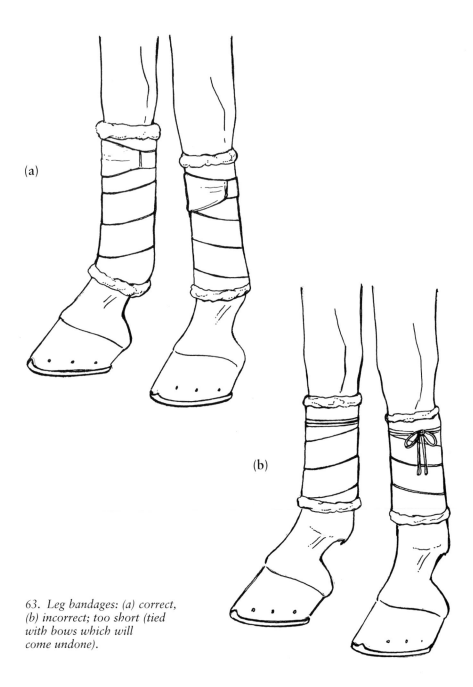

(a)

(b)

63. Leg bandages: (a) correct,
(b) incorrect; too short (tied
with bows which will
come undone).

Bandages These are more difficult to apply and you must make sure that
the pressure is even. Always use something under them, such as Gamgee
or Fibregee, and do not use elastic bandages. Remove the tapes and sew
to secure.

64. Rider and horse ready for the cross-country.

Shells and bandaging Shells are a form of polystyrene shaped to fit round the leg and secured with bandages. They must be trimmed and fitted to the individual leg and used according to the instructions, with one side fitting into a groove made on the other side to stop them being too tight.

THE RIDER

Use the same crash hat as for show jumping, but you can choose the colour of its cover. Gloves, spurs, body protector (compulsory) and whip as for show jumping.

It is sensible to wear a long-sleeved shirt or jumper, as this gives your arms some protection from grazes if you fall off. Gloves need to be chosen carefully, as the horse is likely to become very sweaty and if it rains as well, control could become very difficult. Leather gloves can be rather slippy, but there are many highly efficient materials on the market.

It is compulsory to wear your medical card on your arm and you are not allowed to start without it. You will be given a card when you register yourself and your horse with the BHTA, and it is vital that you fill it in correctly.

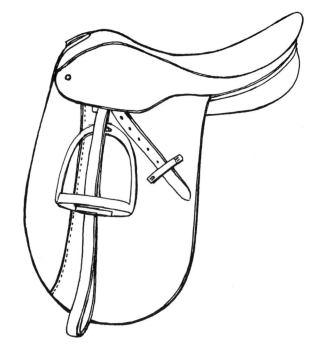

(a)

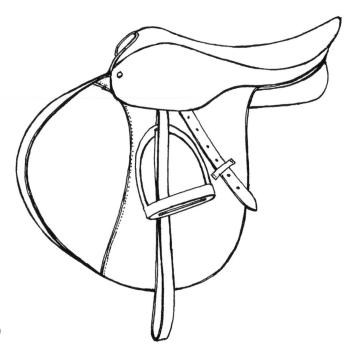

(b)

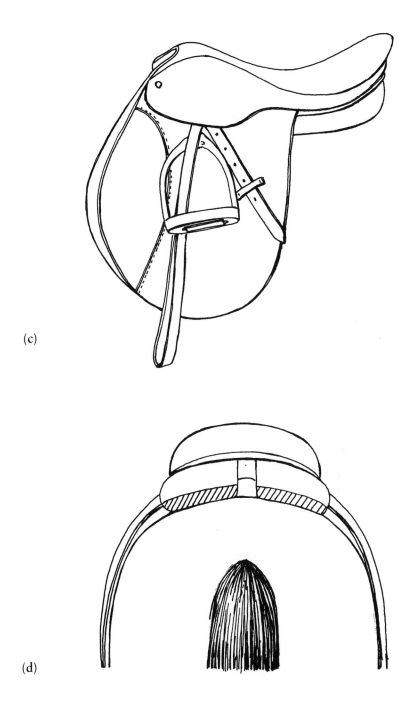

(c)

(d)

65. *Saddles: (a) dressage, (b) cross-country, (c) jumping, (d) broad, flat panels for close contact.*

66. Standing a saddle. Above: *correct, tidy with numnah protecting back of saddle.* Opposite: *incorrect.*

8

One Day or Three: Some General Hints

As mentioned earlier, one-day events may sometimes be spread over two days to cope with the number of entries. You might be asked to do the dressage, and sometimes also the show jumping, on the day before the cross-country. If this is impossible for you, say so on your entry form. However, if you have to travel the day before anyway, you might be happy to get your dressage over with so that you only have the show jumping and cross country to concentrate on the next day. Less tack-changing!

Whichever way you do it, allow plenty of time to warm up before you compete, especially before the cross-country. If you do the dressage on the same day, the horse should already be supple and obedient by the time you jump, but correct preparation is essential.

Remember, too, to look after the people who are with you as either supporters or helpers. Helpers need to be told your plans and starting times so that they know where to be and when. They also need to know what equipment your horse needs, including studs; then they can be left to prepare while you walk the course, collect numbers and generally familiarise yourself with the surroundings. They might also appreciate a snack and a coffee. Ask them to be at the start and finish of each phase to help cope with last-minute panics.

Supporters may have to hang around a lot while you compete, so you can make it more fun for them by telling them your times, suggesting that they walk the cross-country course and involving them in feedback after you have finished. They might even help you by collecting refreshments and scores, which is an added bonus.

Apart from your own 'team', remember that there are a lot of people involved in running an event. Most of them are volunteers, so do be polite, cheerful and cooperative. You are out to enjoy yourself (we hope) so make sure that those running the event enjoy their day too. Afterwards, a letter of thanks to the organisers is always much appreciated.

Three-Day Events

A three-day event involves the same three phases as a one-day, but they are spread over a longer period. If you are just starting out, a three-day event may seem a long way off, but much of the same procedure is used, so learning the routine now will help in the future. One big difference, however, is that the horse does not have to switch quickly from one phase to another, as in a one-day event. Then again, the cross-country is longer, with more time between fences for the horse to switch off and become out of balance. You yourself need to be fitter and more aware of what is coming next.

The four categories of three-day event are:
1*   for Novice horses
2**   for Intermediate horses
3***   for Advanced horses
4****   for experienced Advanced horses

Day 1	Horse inspection: a compulsory check of all horses to make sure that they are fit to compete.
Days 2 and 3	Dressage. Depending on the number of entries, this may take two days.
Day 4	Speed and endurance. This day has four phases (see below).
Day 5	Final horse inspection; show jumping.

Dressage
Preparing to ride your dressage test at a three-day event is made easier by the fact that you have already been there for a day or two, so the horse has had time to settle in and get used to the surroundings. Also, having one day solely devoted to the dressage means that you can concentrate on the test.

The test is normally a little longer than at a one-day event, but still contains appropriate movements for the particular level. Generally there are two or three judges, and the scores are all added together then divided by the number of judges.

Cross-Country
The running order
Phase A. Roads and tracks, to be ridden at a speed of 220 metres per minute.
Phase B. Steeplechase, to be ridden at 640-690 metres per minute, depending on the level of the event.

Phase C. Roads & tracks, speed as Phase A.

Phase D. Cross-country, to be ridden at 520-570 metres per minute, depending on the level of the event.

Roads & Tracks

Phases A and C usually take place over varied terrain, but are well marked with both kilometre and direction signs. Phase A is designed as a warm-up for the horse before the stresses of the steeplechase, and normally lasts between 15 and 30 minutes. Phases A and C are both ridden at the same speed, 220 metres per minute, which for most horses is an active trot or steady canter. If you choose to walk you have to move quite swiftly to catch up on time.

An average of four minutes per kilometre gives you time for a little walk at the end of both phases. When you drive round the track beforehand, assess the state of the ground and work out where to go steady and where to make up time. The clock runs on from phase A to the finish of phase C, so you must aim to arrive at the end of phase A with two minutes to spare in order to get your bearings, tighten your girth and start phase B.

The Steeplechase

This normally has six to eight fences to be jumped at between 640 and 690 metres per minute, depending on the level. The speed is testing for the horse, and over-stressing him at this stage will affect his fitness to complete the cross country. Rhythm and understanding of pace are a great asset. The finish posts of phase B are the start of phase C, which is the second roads and tracks.

There will be an assistance point some distance from the finish, which will be marked and shown to you on the drive round phases A and C. At this point there will be water available, as well as a farrier in case your horse loses a shoe. Your assistant must be there, but it is best not to stop unless you have a problem as the clock keeps on ticking and you would have to make up for the lost time. However, in very hot conditions it is a good idea for your assistant to quickly sponge the horse with cold water.

The Cross-Country

In this phase the course is considerably longer than at a one-day event, thus testing the horses' stamina and fitness. Your judgment of pace and rhythm is vital in order to use the horse's fitness and ability to the greatest advantage. There are longer galloping distances between fences, so you must keep alert and concentrating.

You can practise using a stopwatch to get a feeling of your horse's paces. Mark out a distance of about 1km, with markers at 220m (R&T), 520m, 550m, 570m (XC) and 640m, 690m (steeplechase). You can use these markers to familiarise yourself with the speeds at which to ride each phase.

Remember that the roads and tracks speed is attainable by everyone, whereas the cross-country and steeplechase speeds are only attainable by experienced horse and rider combinations, so aim within your limitations. It would be tempting to go too fast at the start and run out of energy, or to start too slowly and find that you cannot catch up on time. Only experience will make you skillful at this. Unfortunately a one-horse rider does not get much opportunity to practise, as two three-day events per year is quite enough for the horse.

The Show Jumping
This phase takes place on the final day. Rather than testing the horse's ability to jump great heights, it is designed to see if he has recovered his balance and athleticism after the previous day's cross-country exertion. Normally the show jumping course has plenty of space and the jumps are positioned to encourage forward riding, but many horses and riders dread it because they have to approach it so carefully. A long, low, flat stride will result in a flat jump and cost you faults.

When you work in for this phase, concentrate on suppling the horse and shortening his canter strides after the galloping of the cross-country. Be careful not to overdo the practice jumping, though, as the horse will be physically tired, even if he appears to be mentally bright.

9

How to Tackle a Three-Day Event

At a three-day event there is more time for the course walking and riding-in, but it is very easy to waste time. Dressage normally runs over two days, so with the horse inspection on day one, two days of dressage, one day of cross-country and one of show jumping, you actually have a five-day event.

If you live some distance from the venue it makes sense to arrive a day early to get your horse settled into the stables and sort out your groom's and your own accommodation. This is easier if you are lucky enough to have a horsebox with living space, as long as you bring along plenty of food, dry clothing, wet weather gear and all the necessities for your horse while away from home for a week. Be prepared for all weather.

Some three-day events offer caravan space for riders or grooms at a reasonable cost, which allows you to remain on site. Staying at a local B&B will involve arranging extra transport, and will only be viable if you have an experienced groom who can remain in charge of your horse. There is not always a choice of stable bedding. Usually only straw is available, but most events provide wood shavings at extra cost. If you have other preferences, you may want to take your own bedding.

On arrival at a three-day event you must produce your horse's vaccination certificate or passport, which will be checked against him before he is admitted to the stables. He will also be checked for general health, such as coughing or runny nose. Once you and your horse are settled in, you can plan the rest of the week.

Day 1

Much of your time will be taken up with the competitors' briefing and driving and walking the courses, so it is important to get up in time to exercise your horse first. This can normally only be done in a restricted area as you will not yet know exactly where you are allowed to ride. Sometimes, but not always, the roads & tracks course can be used.

At the briefing you will be told about any special rules, changes to the programme, the cross-country course, areas in which you are allowed to exercise and any other information not already provided.

Drive round phases A and C, roads & tracks; walk round the steeplechase, phase B, and cross-country, phase D. These two are usually unescorted but there will often be a short briefing at the start to point out things like the starting box, method of starting, waiting area at start of phase B and assistance area at end of phase B, layout of 'D' box and positioning of water, farrier, ice and loo.

There may also be a different area at the end of the cross-country for cooling off and washing down your horse. This may be monitored by a steward, and the horse may be checked by a vet before he leaves the area and returns to the stables.

The Horse Inspections

At a three-day event there are two horse examinations and three horse inspections. The examinations take place (a) on arrival at the event and (b) after phase D. The inspections are as follows:

1 The first inspection, or trot-up, takes place before the dressage (usually the afternoon before), after the competitors' briefing. It is conducted by the ground jury and veterinary delegate and horses are inspected in hand, at rest and in movement. The aim is to establish that horses are sound and in suitable physical condition to compete. Once your horse has passed the Inspection you will be declared a starter and soon afterwards you will receive your dressage times, so you can then plan for the next two days.

2 The second inspection takes place after phase C at the start of the 10-minute halt. This is conducted by a committee or panel consisting of a member of the ground jury and the vet. The aim is to ensure that horses are fit, sound and in a safe condition to start phase D.

3 The third (and final) inspection takes place on the morning of the show jumping and is conducted by the same committee and under the same conditions as the first inspection. This is to establish that horses are in a fit condition to undertake the jumping test after the rigours of the speed and endurance phases.

The first and third inspections are carried out in exactly the same way, with the horse presented by the competitor. In very exceptional circumstances you can delegate someone else to present the horse, but it is good manners for the competitor to be the presenter.

The second inspection is designed to interfere as little as possible. It is wise to allow extra time for the final kilometre of phase C so the horse can walk the last section and come into the 10-minute box cool and breathing quietly. Trot the last 20 metres into the Box so that the panel can check for soundness. The horse should then stand and the rider may dismount, but helpers may not take the horse away. The panel will ask for the horse to be walked away, where a vet may check his pulse, respiration and temperature. The rider should be prepared to be either recalled after five minutes or told to continue.

The trot-up

1 You should present your horse looking as good as possible – clean, tidy and plaited. If you don't have a groom, allow plenty of time to prepare.
2 Rider turnout should be immaculate and suitable, especially footwear: i.e. do wear shoes that you can run in.
3 The horse should be sound, bright, alert and moving actively.
4 The horse should be presented to the ground jury standing square. The best way to achieve this is to stand facing the horse, slightly to near side. Your left hand on the right rein a few inches from the bit will help control while your right hand is holding the buckle and left rein a few inches from the bit. Your eye should be firmly fixed on the horse.

The horse should be trained to walk off in a brisk march for five or six strides then to do a smart transition into trot, continuing to the end of the trot-up arena (which will be marked, but you should reconnoitre the area first). At the turn point, make a smart transition to walk in a straight line, make the turn in walk, do another smart transition into trot and continue past the ground jury. They will then announce pass, fail or hold.

'Hold' means that you will be escorted to be examined by another vet, who is there to help clear any doubts that the ground jury may have. He or she will advise the ground jury, who will then make another inspection and a final decision. If necessary you may be assisted by one of your helpers – for example, putting on a rug.

A few important points
- Establish the trot-up location on arrival. It may be a long way from the stables. Arrive in plenty of time to give your horses a good walk or trot around to take in the atmosphere.
- A horse looks and moves better if his spine, from ears to tail, is in a straight line.
- He must be walked and trotted in a straight line. Fixing your eye on a distant point and running towards it may help you.
- Do not turn and look at your horse.

- Most horses trot best with the leader just in front of their shoulder, left hand holding the rein buckle, right hand under the horse's chin or 10ins from the bit, with a loose rein.
- Each horse has a tempo and stride at which he looks best. Train at home to discover his best pace and teach him to respond to your 'trot' and 'walk' commands.
- It is important to warm up your horse for about 10 minutes before the trot-up.
- Feet should be picked out just beforehand, and any boots or bandages removed.
- The horse should wear a snaffle bridle.

67. The trot-up at a three-day event.

Day 2: First Dressage Day

If this is your dressage day, decide how many times your horse needs to go out before his test. Depending on your time and his temperament you could take him out early, put him away to settle, then get him out again nearer to the test.

Whatever happens, don't forget to fit in a course walk, as although you may have the second day free it is surprising how much there is to do. And remember that having performed his test on day one, it is very important for the horse to keep up a normal level of exercise on day two. You cannot store his energy by giving him a light day and if he has not been sufficiently worked you may run into trouble and find that he ties up on cross-country day.

He will also need a 'pipe opener' and possibly a jump in order to get his heart and lungs working and stretch the muscles that were not used in the dressage. This jump is not to train him – which should have been done already – but to have some fun and allow you both to get your eye in.

Day 3: Second Dressage Day

If your dressage is on the second day you will have schooled and exercised your horse on day one, but it is probably best to leave the pipe-opener and jump until after the dressage. You must press on and do plenty of course walking, both steeplechase and cross-country, so that you don't end up rushing around at the last minute. Another task on dressage day is to prepare equipment for the 10-minute box, which is explained more fully on page 106.

Essentials
Appropriate rugs, such as sweat rug, winter cooler, waterproof
Buckets, 2 sponges, sweat-scraper
Towels
Spare girth, bridle, stirrup-leather, whip, gloves
Spare boots
Simple first aid kit
Studs
Spare set of shoes with appropriate studs already in
Scissors
Grease and rubber glove
Hoof pick
Hole punch
Spare tape

68. *Tack and other items needed in the 10-minute box.*

Jacket for rider
Drink for rider
Plan of fences

Day 4: Speed and Endurance

It is important to feed your horse early enough to give him several hours to digest his breakfast, which must not be too heavy. However, because of the way his digestive system works, and because he needs nutrition for the job in hand, he must not be without food for too long. If you have a late starting time, he may need a small, early lunch as well. Three hours before

105

he starts is early enough to feed. He should have access to water at all times, but hay is not a good idea, as long as he has regular small feeds.

Warming up is very important, so if you have a late time you need to either lead him out for 30 minutes in the morning, or hack him about. This allows him to use his muscles and loosen up in a relaxed way. Once you have a starting time, plan backwards. You need ample time for preparing tack, leg protection and studs, as well as a relaxed warm-up before phase A. The shorter phase A is, the longer the warm-up you will need before it. If it is only 15 minutes, this alone would not be enough warm-up before galloping round the steeplechase, so be prepared to give him a slow build-up towards phase A.

Your helper at the finish of A and start of B (same place) is mainly there to give moral support – no spare parts should be necessary at this stage. Do check your girth and the length of your stirrups. Once you start, your helpers must get to the assistance point at the end of phase B, which is also the start of phase C. At this stage they should bring a spare set of shoes, reins and a stirrup leather, just in case. Do not stop at this stage unless you have a problem because the clock ticks on, using up the time allowed. If you need to replace a shoe a farrier is available, and he will put it on as quickly as possible.

In very hot weather a swift cooling down session may be useful: plenty of cold water applied to the horse's neck and body, and a drink for the rider.

Get the routine down to a fine art, as time wasted at this stage will mean the horse has to make a greater effort to catch up on the clock.

The 10-minute box

At the end of phase C (roads & tracks) and before the start of phase D (cross-country), you come into the 10-minute box, where there is a compulsory 10-minute rest for horse and rider. You will be required to trot the last 20 yards into it, with a vet and ground jury members watching.

Here the horse is assessed by a vet and a member of the ground jury for soundness and fitness to continue. Other checks such as temperature and respiration may also be made, but this is all standard procedure and nothing to worry about. Should any of these readings be abnormal, the horse will be rechecked after five minutes, by which time things will probably have settled down. Sometimes a fast heartbeat may be due to excitement and will soon return to normal. However, if the vet is still concerned at this stage he may advise you not to continue. You would be wise to accept his advice and to realise that it is given to protect the safety of you and your horse, and that there is always another day.

Once this inspection is over, you will have a chance to check tack,

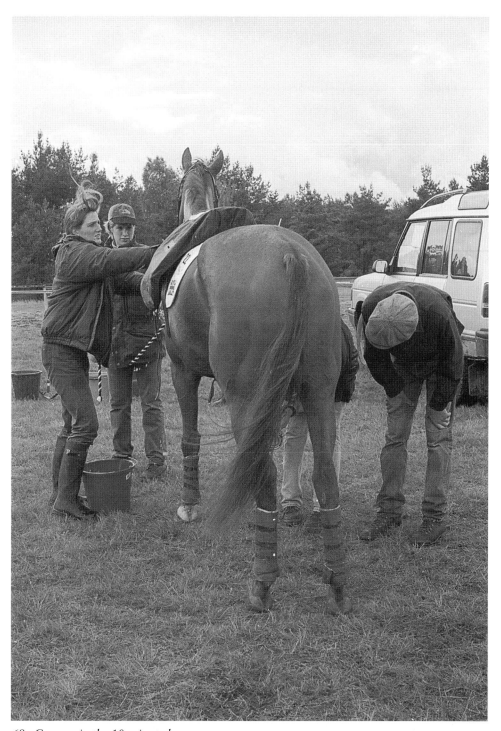

69. *Grooms in the 10-minute box.*

studs, boots and bandages, wash the horse down if he needs cooling off, put on a rug to keep him warm if necessary and generally check his well-being. He must be kept moving for most of the time so that his muscles remain loose and warm. Too much standing still can do more harm than good.

Changing the studs in his shoes is not a good idea at this stage, as standing on three legs puts uneven strain on his muscles. A highly-strung horse could cause problems and a nervous helper might not get the studs in correctly. By the time all four sets have been changed most of the 10 minutes could be up.

In the 10-minute box efficient helpers are very useful, since this leaves you free to collect your thoughts, visit the loo or just relax for a moment. A copy of the course plan, probably in the programme, is also handy, especially if there are pictures of the fences. This all helps to concentrate your mind. Your helpers can be best used if one is responsible for holding the horse, then leading it around, while one or two others do anything else that is necessary.

Some horses have a tendency to become very stiff in their muscles during the 10-minute break. This is commonly known as 'tying up', and is a metabolic fault which has many causes, the most usual being inappropriate feeding or an inconsistent exercise programme. Any sign of muscle stiffness requires professional advice.

Helpers' routine in the 10-minute box
All this takes time, especially if you have not done it before, so it's a good idea to practise and, as mentioned earlier, to prepare your equipment the day before.

- ❑ Loosen girths (but do not remove saddle), run up the stirrups, bring the reins over the horse's head and rug him up if necessary. Do not cover a hot horse on a hot day, as trapping heat will not allow his temperature to return to normal.
- ❑ Wash the horse down with a suitable amount of water for the weather conditions, scrape him off and walk him round until it is time for the rider to remount.
- ❑ Check his leg protection and studs but preferably do not change them.
- ❑ Check his shoes.
- ❑ After five minutes, set the saddle forward, tighten girths, then lead him round again.
- ❑ Apply grease to front of fore and hind legs but not to his chest, as this is where horses lose heat by sweating so it must not be clogged up with grease.

❑ Wipe reins and stirrup irons with a towel in case they are wet.

❑ Leg up the rider and, before they put their feet in the stirrups, wipe the soles of their boots with a towel to prevent slipping.

❑ Make sure that the rider is concentrating and guide them to the start of phase D.

❑ When your horse first moves off from standing, check that he is not stiff in the hind legs. If he is, seek professional advice as he may be about to tie up.

Finishing the course

At the end of the cross-country pull up gradually, as a sudden halt puts strain on the horse's tendons. You must remain in the finishing area, where a vet keeps an eye on each horse until permission is given to leave. Once you are off the horse it is a good idea to keep him moving as much as possible. Wash him down but then move him around, as horses cool by a process of evaporation. Do not allow him to eat, but a small drink straight away is good, then offer regular drinks of about a quarter of a bucket every 15 minutes. Remove tack and leg protection but keep him moving until his breathing is back to normal.

On returning to the stable

Check the horse's legs for injuries and seek professional help if necessary. There will always be a vet in the stable area to help you. If all appears well, it is best either to dry bandage or to leave legs uncovered for a couple of hours.

One hour after completion

This is about the right time to give the horse a small, easily digestible feed and a small haynet. He is normally hungry by now but don't overdo it – you probably wouldn't want to eat a three-course meal yourself at this stage. Leave him in peace for a couple of hours to rest and relax.

About three hours after completion

Reassess the horse's condition. Take off the bandages, lead him out for a stroll and possibly a graze for about 15 minutes, then give him a trot and see how he looks. If all appears well, then a little more walking is valuable before he goes back to the stable. Now apply cooling paste, kaolin or dry bandages – whichever you prefer, but do not use anything that you have not tried before in case he is allergic to it. If you finish early in the day, he will probably need a second walk later on. Then leave him to have a good night's rest.

You must now think about day five. You may be able to walk the show

70. Cooling off after the cross-country.

jumping course on the evening of cross-country day – you will be told about this at the briefing – and may even be able to wear whatever clothing you choose (within reason!). On show jumping day you must dress correctly for all course-walking unless told otherwise.

Sample time-card

This is based on a two-star three-day event, but is a guide only, as the distances vary at every event. However, if you keep a copy it will help you work out your next card.

A roads & tracks speed of 220 metres per minute works out at about four minutes per kilometre, allowing time for an arrival at the finish at least one minute before the allotted time. Timings of kilometre markers may vary according to the state of the ground and to how your horse is feeling.

Start your stopwatch:
- at the start of phase A and stop it at the end of A
- at the start of B and keep running until the end of C
- at the start of D

Your card can be on actual event time or start at 0.

Start A:	00		1 min compulsory halt	*Start C:*	3 mins 30 secs	
1km	4 mins		*Start B:* 00	1km	9 mins	
2km	8 mins			2km	13 mins	
3km	12 mins		*Finish B:* 3 mins 30 secs	3km	17 mins	
4km	16 mins		*Start C:* 3 mins 30 secs	4km	21 mins	
Finish A: 19 mins				5km	25 mins	
Time allowed			Time allowed	6km	29 secs	
20 mins			3 mins 30 secs	7km	33 secs	
				Time allowed		
				34 mins 30 secs		
				+3½ mins = 38 mins		
				(1 min in hand)		

Start D:	00
Half way around course	5 mins
Finish D:	10 mins

A sample of a card for a rider on cross-country day at a three-day event, giving times and km markers.

Start A:	11.06am	1 min compulsory halt	*Start C:*	11.30.30am	
1km	11.10	*Start B:* 11.27	1km	11.36	
2km	11.14		2km	11.40	
3km	11.18	*Finish B:* 11.30.30	3km	11.44	
4km	11.22	*Start C:* 11.30.30	4km	11.48	
Finish A: 11.25			5km	11.52	
Time allowed 20 mins		Time allowed	6km	11.56	
Due in at 11.26am		3 mins 30 secs	7km	12.00	
			Finish C: 12.04		
			Due in	12.05pm	
			Time allowed		
			34 mins 30 secs		

10 mins compulsory halt	
Start D:	12.15pm
Half-way round course	12.20
Finish D:	12.25

71. Stopwatch attached to the rider's glove with Velcro.

Final Day: The Show Jumping

You will need to make an early start so that you can asses your horse's condition and proceed accordingly. Remember to organise everything you do to suit the time of the final inspection.

First, remove any leg protection or paste and hose off the horse's legs if necessary so that you can have a good look at them. Then lead him around in walk until he is loosened up – it is quite normal for a horse to be a little stiff at first. After this, trot him to see how he really moves.

Hopefully he will be fine, but consult the vet on duty if you have any serious doubts. The vet is there to help you, and this will not detract from any decisions at the final inspection.
Some horses loosen up better if you tack up and go for a gentle hack.

Having made your initial assessment, it is probably best to return the horse to the stable and feed him, then groom and plait him before exercising him, either ridden or in hand, directly before the trot-up. Do not present him sweaty, as this may make the panel suspicious. Allow time for a final tidy-up and to pick out feet.

Once you have crossed this hurdle, focus your mind on the show jumping. Walk the course and work out your approximate jumping time, then work backwards from it to give yourself sufficient time to warm up your horse without exhausting him. Remember that he has worked hard the day before so may be full of adrenaline but not really feeling too athletic.

Do not over-jump him at the practice fence – save his main efforts for the arena.

After the show jumping and – with luck – the prize giving, do not abandon all responsibility for your horse. He now needs time to relax and to be prepared for the journey home. Do not rush this. Allow time, too, to comfortably give him water and a feed before loading up. If you have a very long journey it is better to stay another night and travel home when you both feel fresher.

10

After the Event

You need more than one successful run at each level before you move up. At first you might make good progress, but at some time a problem is bound to occur, and how you cope with this may be the key to your future. Wherever the problem occurs, you must analyse both the problem and the cause, then eliminate the cause and progress carefully.

For example, if you have been going rather fast on the cross-country, your horse may hardly have had time to see what he has jumped. One day he may make a mistake and either fall or give himself a fright, which could make him look more carefully next time and question his own ability and bravery. It is always best to start the cross-country slowly and build up speed with confidence. Slowly does not mean not going forward, but it does mean riding the horse in a rhythmical, balanced, controlled and forward pace suitable for the type of obstacle ahead. This allows the horse to see what he is jumping and to remain relaxed and confident.

In dressage it can be a temptation to force the less experienced horse into an outline. This means pulling his head and neck into shape, which may fool some people – but not many judges will accept it and, as your horse progresses, all sorts of pitfalls will arise. The horse must learn to move forward from the hind leg into the rein, and you must allow his muscles to develop enough to carry his weight further back on his hind quarters.

Whether you have finished a three-day event or a series of one-days, if the horse is now going to have a holiday you cannot just turn him out. You need to change his routine and feeding programme gradually. He will probably be very happy to spend time in the field, but horses are creatures of habit so if he is not used to going out he needs time to adjust. You could start with one hour and progress according to the weather, his health and the state of the grass. If there is a lot of rich grass available he will need time to get used to it, whereas no grass and a muddy field will lead him to seek alternative activities such as charging about.

It is advisable to hack your horse for about a week as you change his diet and exercise plan. Keep a strict eye on his legs, especially if you have any worries about his soundness; often strains and sprains do not show up immediately but may take four or five days to become evident.

How long a holiday you give your horse depends largely on your long-term plans. If he is fit and well, six weeks can be plenty, or sometimes it can be less. A change from constant training is a good idea, but it is unwise to let him get too fat or unfit, which can easily happen during summer breaks. These can be kept shorter, with perhaps a longer break after the autumn events.

Once the horse has had a break and has come back into fitness this is a good time to work on his athletic ability in the show jumping. You can both learn a great deal by going to pure show jumping competitions, indoor and outdoor, to gain experience in course jumping, ring craft and quick thinking.

Making plans for eventing means being prepared to reassess and reschedule regularly. Having an initial long-term plan is good, but your horse's performance and soundness will often spoil it and you must be prepared to let these factors guide you. If more low-level events are needed, they will benefit both of you in the long term. This is a good time to take stock of the both horse and your own performance and discuss plans with your trainer or advisor. Do not be deterred by setbacks – analyse their causes and, if necessary, go back to basics. Learn by your mistakes but do not be over ambitious after one good result – consolidate it, and only progress when the foundation is firm and your confidence high.

72. *What it's all about: concentration and determination.*

11

A Final Note on Training

There are many roads to Rome, it is said, and therefore there is more than one way of training your horse – but from the start there are some basic rules which will stand you in good stead for the future.

1. The 'engine' of your horse is his hind legs, so you must always remember to ride forward from the leg to the rein.

2. You must not shorten the horse's neck by pulling it in. The neck contributes to balance and can only be effective when the hind legs are engaged and weight-bearing. This process is only achieved with time and patience. The horse has to learn to adjust his weight and maintain his own balance. The rein must not become a 'fifth leg': it is important for the rider to learn to have an elastic contact on the rein and to be able to stabilise the contact between the hand and the horse's mouth.

3. There are two important lines for the rider to think of in dressage: elbow-wrist-horse's mouth and shoulder-hip-heel.

In your preparation for competing in horse trials, it is important not only to work on the three main phases but also to look upon the work as an overall training, each phase complementing the others. A supple, obedient, confident, trained horse can succeed where a more talented but less well prepared horse may fail. The flatwork is the basis for everything, so take your time and be patient, and try to make everything enjoyable for both you and the horse.

Most horses can achieve a reasonable result up to novice level, but in order to reach higher levels they need a certain temperament, enthusiasm and physical ability. At pre-novice and novice level you can get great enjoyment and satisfaction from an overall solid performance.

Training is important at any stage, from basic safety to top level results. To achieve good results you need to reach a very high standard in all three phases. It is therefore possible to enjoy this sport at grass roots level, where you can be competing with top riders who are trying out their less experienced horses. This means that you will have the chance to learn a lot by watching your fellow competitors.

Appendix A

The BHTA levels

Pre-Novice (Grade 3) is the starting point at senior level. Horses must not have any points before they start, and there is no prize money or points to be won. Courses are designed for first-timers to gain experience.

Cross-country fences	Up to 1.08m (3ft 6ins) high
	Max base spread of 2.10m (6ft 11ins)
	Max top spread 1.20m (3ft 11ins)
Running speed	490 metres per minute.
Show jumps	Up to 1.10m (3ft 7ins)
Dressage	A simple test to show good basic training, with the horse's outline not being forced and the natural paces being looked after, not stifled. A fluent, forward-going test with the horse relaxed and happy is ideal. Trot work can be executed rising or sitting.

Novice (Grade 3) comes next. You are ready for this when you and your horse are going clear, safely and confidently round pre-novice courses, and you leave it when your horse has gained 21 points. Although the cross-country fence dimensions are the same as pre-novice, there will be more challenges such as combinations and narrow fences. Remember, it's not always the *size* of a jump that causes trouble, but the *siting* of it. There are penalties for going too fast and it is better to gain experience by going clear at a steady pace. If you go too fast too soon and make mistakes you risk your confidence as well as that of your horse.

Cross-country fences	Up to 1.08m (3ft 6ins) high
	Max base spread of 2.10m (6ft 11ins)
	Max top spread 1.20m (3ft 11ins)

Running speed	520 metres per minute (slightly faster than pre-novice)
Show jumps	Up to 1.15m (3ft 9ins)
Dressage	As pre-novice, but starting to progress to some lengthening of the paces.

Open Novice is for horses with fewer than 36 points, since the cross-country is still novice standard although the dressage and show jumping are intermediate.

Cross-country fences	Up to 1.08m (3ft 6ins) high
	Max base spread of 2.10m (6ft 11ins)
	Max top spread 1.20m (3ft 11ins)
Running speed	520 metres per minute.
Show jumps	Up to 1.20m (3ft 11ins)
Dressage	Includes instant transitions, counter-canter, some medium paces, rein-back and the start of lateral work. This is preparing the horse for the next level – intermediate – and is similar to an elementary test in pure dressage.

Intermediate is for horses and riders with considerable experience who have both achieved five clear rounds at novice level, though not necessarily as a pair. Horses can stay in intermediate until they have 60 points.

Open Intermediate is open to all grades, including advanced horses who sometimes need a confidence-giving run at a lower level than they are qualified for.

Cross-country fences	Up to 1.15m (3ft 9ins) high
	Max base spread 2.45m (8ft)
	Max top spread 1.60m (5ft 3ins)
Running speed	570 metres per minute
Show jumps	Up to 1.20m (3ft 11ins)
Dressage	As above

Advanced Intermediate is also open to all grades, with advanced dressage and show jumping but intermediate cross-country. This is designed for less experienced horses but is not suitable for less experienced riders. You need to consolidate your skills at intermediate level before you try this one.

Cross-country fences	Up to 1.15m (3ft 9ins) high
	Max base spread 2.45m (8ft)
	Max top spread 1.60m (5ft 3ins)
Running speed	570 metres per minute
Show jumps	Up to 1.25m (4ft 1in)
Dressage	Good self-carriage; working, medium and extended paces; half-pass; counter-canter. This would be similar to a medium test in pure dressage.

Advanced is for horses with 61 points or more. Intermediate horses are also eligible if they have five clear rounds across country at intermediate level. The dressage tests are regularly updated and may include new movements.

Cross-country fences	Up to 1.20m (3ft 11ins) high
	Max base spread 2.80m (9ft 2ins)
	Max top spread 1.80m (5ft 11ins)
Running speed	600 metres per minute
Show jumps	Up to 1.25m (4ft 1in)
Dressage	As advanced intermediate, but now introducing flying changes in canter. Comparable to advanced medium in pure dressage.

Appendix B

Administration, Registration and Entries

To compete in British Horse Trials Association (BHTA) affiliated events, the horse, rider and owner must all be registered. These registrations run for a year, though half-year registrations are available after 31 July.

First of all there is paperwork to be done. Choose a name for your horse that has not already been registered (to save time, the BHTA will often help you over the telephone by looking up their database of names).

An up-to-date vaccination certificate, with a diagrammatic description of your horse, is absolutely vital and you must take it with you to all affiliated events. If you cannot produce it when asked, you may not be allowed to compete. If it has lapsed, the whole course of injections has to be started again and your horse will not be allowed to compete until at least seven days after his second injection. It is a good idea to keep a photocopy of the certificate at home for reference.

Then you need to register the horse with the British Horse Database (BHD), which aims to record the breeding and performance of all competition horses in order to help breeders produce high class competition horses in the future. You must use the name you have registered rather than the horse's stable name. His passport or diagrammatic vaccination certificate will then be stamped with a sticker confirming his name and BHD number.

Now register yourself as a member of the BHTA, and register the horse's owner if he is owned by someone else. You will be given a membership number. Forms can be obtained from head office.

Next, register your horse with the BHTA, using the same name recorded with the BHD. He will be known by that name for all horse trials records. At the same time, purchase a blank number bib. At each event you will be given A4-size number sheets to insert into the bib. You must also wear the medical card, fully completed, secured to your arm for the cross-country phase; some body protectors have a special pocket on the shoulder pad for these. This is vital, as it holds all the information a medical team may need in case of emergency.

All these instructions are given in the Rule Book and Omnibus Schedule, which you receive when you join the BHTA. You must be aware of the rules relating to your competition, as it is your responsibility to know what is and what is not allowed. Carry the Rule Book with you for reference, along with your vaccination certificate, medical card, number bib and a copy of your start times.

Once you have registered, you will receive a card with your horse's allotted number and this, along with your own registration number, is to be used on every entry form. You will also be sent a set of special ballot labels stating your horse's name, registration number and the period in which the labels can be used. This ensures that when you use a ballot label you will be given priority to compete in every ballot period, as laid out in the omnibus schedule. The omnibus schedule is the only official publication giving details of all the affiliated horse trials in the country with relevant information for each event, so don't lose it! From it your whole season's eventing will be planned. Entry forms will also be sent with your registration documents. Do study the forms before you fill them in, as any that are not correctly filled in may be rejected, jeopardising your chance to compete.

Work carefully through the entry form. As information required for different events may be similar, it is worth making up a crib-sheet for quick reference. If you can, photocopy the form so that you have a record of the information you have given.

Entries must be received at least a month before the event, so plan carefully, especially if you are trying to qualify for a particular series or prize. If a class is over-subscribed, a balloting system operates, but entries received with a special ballot label in the top right-hand corner are accepted first. Occasionally there are too many special ballot labels and these have to be balloted too – but if you fail to gain an entry you are most unlucky, as normally Event Secretaries try to give everyone a chance. However, any entry form that has to be returned for amendment will almost certainly lose its place, so it is worth spending time getting your form right.

Send an SAE with your entry for the Secretary to return your acceptance, which gives your competitor number and section start times, as well as the phone number to ring for your personal start times. You will receive the note about a week before the event, and will be told when to phone for times – often it will be as late as the night before the class. You can work out approximate dressage times by noting how many are in your section and where your number lies in comparison, allowing about five minutes per test. If times are not available until the night before, at least this gives you a rough idea of when you will need to leave home.

Above all, if you need to phone the Event Secretary, be sure to do so at a reasonable time, with reasonable requests, and do be polite – most of these people give their time voluntarily, so the least you can do is be nice to them!

Checklist

For the rider
Riding hat with relevant hat covers
Hairnet
Gloves
Whips for each phase
Gumshield
Riding jacket
Waterproof jacket
Body protector
Cross-country top
Jodhpurs/breeches
Stock and stock pin
Stock shirt
Riding boots
Spurs
Stop watch
Medical armband
Number bib
BHTA Rule Book

For the horse
Vaccination certificate
Travel boots/leg protection
Sweat rug, summer sheet or appropriate rugs
Show jumping and cross-country leg protection
Insulating tape
Buckets and water
Sweat scraper and sponges
Saddle and bridle
Martingale and breastplate
Cross-country surcingle
Towel
2 x bindertwine
Feed and hay
Studs and kit
Grooming kit
First aid kits for horse and rider
Spare set of shoes

Index